Journey Into Ice

John Franklin and the Northwest Passage

Picture Credits

With the exception of those particularly noted below, the pictures in *Journey Into Ice* are from Library of Congress prints made from books by Franklin, Flinders, and Beechey, and a few others—all now out of print—most of which are listed in the Bibliography on page 257.

For the pictures from other sources, the authors and publisher are grateful to the following for permission to reproduce:

Pictures on pages 13, 16, 17, 23, 67, 83, and 250, Courtesy, National Maritime Museum, Greenwich, England; and, on page 205, Courtesy, National Maritime Museum, Greenwich Hospital, Greenwich, England.

Pictures on pages 28 and 29, Courtesy, The American Museum of Natural History, New York, N.Y.

Picture on page 87, Courtesy, The Mariners Museum, Newport News, Va.

Picture on page 89, Courtesy, National Park Service, U.S. Department of Interior.

Picture of Franklin on the jacket, and pictures on pages 105, 162, 188, 215, and 254, Courtesy, Trustees of the British Museum, London.

Pictures on pages 107 and 174, Courtesy, Hudson's Bay Company, Winnipeg, Manitoba, Canada.

Picture on page 190, Courtesy, Queen Victoria Museum, Launceston, Tasmania.

Picture on page 195, Courtesy, Australian News and Information Bureau, New York, N.Y.

Pictures on pages 223, 230, and 237, Courtesy, National Portrait Gallery, London.

Picture on page 225, Courtesy, Royal Geographical Society, London.

Pictures on pages 252 and 253, Courtesy, Norwegian Information Service, New York.

The photographs on pages 197 and 212 are by Don Stephens, Hobart, Tasmania; and the maps were prepared especially for this book, and are Copyright by Rand McNally & Co.

Journey Into Ice

John Franklin and the Northwest Passage

by Ann and Myron Sutton

ILLUSTRATED WITH PHOTOGRAPHS AND MAPS

Rand McNally & Company

Chicago · New York · San Francisco

To Arthur Stupka

CONTENTS

ILLUSTRATIONS

MAPS

INTRODUCTION

The discovery of the Northwest Passage, said Samuel Purchas, a seventeenth-century compiler of travel books, is the only "thing yet undone wherebye a notable mind might be made famous."

For hundreds of years men hunted the Northwest Passage, an icy and dangerous route by sea among the islands of northern Canada. Through howling gales and churning seas they steered their sailing ships in search of a way to fabled Cathay, or China, but without success.

Then came John Franklin, of the English Navy. His was a life of sailing, excitement, and exploration. He fought in three of the most famous battles in history— Copenhagen, Trafalgar, and New Orleans. He helped guide a battered exploring ship on the first voyage around Australia. He survived shipwreck in an unknown sea, sailed toward the North Pole, and finally traveled by ship, canoe, and snowshoe into the frozen wilderness of Canada —where he vanished in one of the strangest mysteries of the Arctic.

In the seven years this book has been in preparation, letters, diaries, journals, and ships' logs have been examined, and the narrative is based on these. So is the dialogue, often as reported in letters of the time, such as the shooting of the *Aigle* sharpshooter and the interview with Lord Haddington.

Spelling of geographic features is generally that of the present day, except for terms like "Polar Sea," which Franklin constantly used in referring to unknown Arctic seas.

For help, the authors are grateful to the following: in Great Britain—the Public Record Office, British Museum, Royal Society, Royal Geographic Society, National Maritime Museum, and National Portrait Gallery; in Australia—the Australian National Travel Association, Queen Victoria Museum and Art Gallery, Australian News and Information Bureau, and Tasmanian Government Tourist and Immigration Department; in Canada—the Department of Northern Affairs and National Resources, and the Hudson's Bay Company; and in the United States—Charles and Joyce Warren, the Mariners Museum, the Norwegian Embassy, the New York Public Library, and the Libraries of Congress and the Department of Interior.

Our thanks go to Arthur Stupka, of the Great Smoky Mountains of Tennessee and North Carolina, a distinguished explorer himself in natural history. His admiration of Franklin led us to the events behind the discovery of the Northwest Passage—an inspiring story of adventure, courage, and devotion to purpose.

ANN AND MYRON SUTTON
Alexandria, Virginia

One

COPENHAGEN

"Fire!"

Gun by gun, the explosions broke the stillness of Copenhagen harbor.

"Fire!"

Again and again, the noise of cannon blasts sounded across the water and among the hills of Denmark. Smoke filled the bay, almost hiding the stately spires of the city of Copenhagen. Through the smoke, Danish ships began to return the British fire.

With every Boom! the warship *Polyphemus* shuddered and her masts and sails shook violently. With every Boom! the lad on the quarterdeck blinked and started.

"They're returning the fire, sir," he shouted, standing straight at his station. Already his white midshipman's shirt was smudged from the dirt and smoke of the battle.

The young midshipman placed his telescope to his eye. Around the harbor, the cannonade was being taken up by guns on ships and on shore. There must be a thousand guns firing, he thought; maybe more.

There! The clouds of smoke parted for a moment and he saw the warship *Elephant,* Admiral Nelson's ship. She was a proud ship, and Nelson a proud commander. Hardly a red-blooded English boy breathed who would not have fought under him!

Crash! The *Polyphemus* lurched and splinters flew through the air.

The boy heard the rapid running of feet, a clatter of muskets, excited voices, all mingled with the booming of guns below. With every blast, the cannons rumbled as they recoiled across the decks.

He coughed in the thick smoke. His eyes filled with tears and he tried to rub away the stinging lest anyone should see him.

A voice shouted above the tumult. "Ahoy, Franklin."

The boy snapped his head around. Another midshipman had leaped up on the quarterdeck.

"Bell!" he shouted. "What are you doing up here? Are you hurt?"

Bell had lost his big hat and had badly torn his coat. Already the white shirt and stockings were covered with dirt. "Isn't it glorious, Franklin? Our first battle."

"I see precious little of it," John Franklin replied, rubbing the smoke from his eyes. "What's the progress, have you heard?"

"We've lost a gun below, smashed by a Danish shell."

"Anyone hurt?"

"Yes, badly I gather. I'm going down again. Come along?"

A cannonball whizzed over their heads, glanced off the mast and tore with a loud rip through one of the sails.

"Heads up, Mr. Bell!" John shouted. "I can't go below. Two enemy block ships have engaged us. We're in the fire of the shore batteries, too. My job is to keep an eye on their actions."

"How many guns bearing on us?"

Franklin's brown eyes darted with excitement. "A hundred and forty, as I count. Maybe more."

**Nelson and the British fleet being fired on as they passed
Cronenburg Castle on their way to Copenhagen
(from a colored aquatint by R. Dodd)**

The other midshipman swept his hand out toward
the harbor. "Look at it, Mr. Franklin. A battle indeed,
sir! A real day for Nelson and for England! I say, have
you counted the ships, theirs and ours?"

"Every one of them," John replied. His roundish face,
perched awkwardly atop a white scarf, betrayed his
eagerness. As he spoke, his eyebrows lifted quickly. His
cheeks folded into a wide grin. "More ships than ever
you or I saw," he replied, "or even Nelson, I'll bet you.
The enemy has six line-of-battle rigs and at least eleven
floating batteries. We have fifty-one sail—with sixteen of
them line-of-battle."

Satisfied, Bell went below.

The battle grew hotter. So loud was the noise now, John judged that all two thousand guns on both sides must be firing. Guns of the *Polyphemus* kept up a constant din. In the terrifying roar and vibration, John tried to peer through the clouds of smoke. It was no use.

Never in all his fifteen years had he seen or heard anything like this. In those fifteen years no such cannonades had stirred the peaceful countryside around his home in Lincolnshire. Nor had he ever breathed such acrid, suffocating smoke.

Crash! More splinters flew through the air.

A cannonball had struck and buried itself in the deck planking. How many balls from the guns of the *Polyphemus* were striking the enemy, John could not tell.

All was bedlam aboard. Above the roar, the lieutenants shouted firing orders: "Load!" "Run out!" "Prime!" "Fire!"

For more than two hours the guns of the *Polyphemus* launched a deadly hail of balls toward the Danish ships and batteries. By mid-afternoon the smoke thinned a little. The pitch of battle changed. For a moment John listened, puzzled. Then he knew. The Danish guns had ceased to fire.

Not until late afternoon could ship's company be mustered. John watched the men of the *Polyphemus* come on deck. Some staggered with pain. Some had to be carried by their fellow seamen. Some wore bandages.

Out in the harbor, white flags of surrender fluttered from every Danish mast that had not been shot away. Guns of distress boomed from hulls that had not been sunk. A few wrecks burned like giant torches. As the light of day faded, boats from the English vessels searched the harbor for survivors of either side.

The sea lay thickly strewn with broken masts. Pieces of rope and canvas floated among them. Once John had looked overboard and seen through the clear water the bodies of several men on the floor of the bay.

When the muster ended, they found that six men had been killed, among them Franklin's friend, James Bell.

That night, John stood in sadness at the edge of the ship, watching the fires, and listening to the shouts and cries of pain. He had lost a friend and fellow midshipman. The world would be lonely without James Bell.

It would be lonely for others, too. More than a thousand Englishmen had been lost or wounded that day in April, 1801. Six thousand Danes were killed, wounded, or captured.

Admiral Nelson, nearly exhausted, could be proud. He was to speak of this day at Copenhagen as "the most hard-fought battle and the most complete victory that ever was fought and obtained by the navy of this country."

During all his years at school, John had dreamed of exactly this kind of adventure. With a laugh he now remembered how the headmaster at Louth grammar school had caught him peering out the window and thinking of ships instead of numbers.

Away from school he had run wildly—or as wildly as his heavy body permitted—across those rolling hills of Lincolnshire to stand at the edge of the sea. There he had stood and dreamed and prayed that God would help him become a sailor.

Uniforms of Franklin's time: *Top left:* Purser; *Top right:* Sailor; *Lower left:* Cook

Now he was one. Little did he realize then how much of a sailor he would become or to what far ends of the earth he was to go. At the taffrail of the *Polyphemus,* watching the foaming wake of the ship, he let the adventures of Captain James Cook tumble again through his mind. He knew those travels almost by heart. New Zealand . . . Tahiti . . . Antarctica . . . names with strange, wonderful sounds.

John turned and looked up into the masts. The great sails billowed in the wind. He heard the yardarms creak and listened to the breezes singing through the rigging. He smelled the salt spray of the sea and the dankness of the ship's wet timbers. It stirred the blood of the fifteen-year-old midshipman.

As he strode back up on the quarterdeck to check the compass and read the chronometer, his eyes had a faraway look.

"Land ho" came a shout from the crow's nest.

Midshipman

Two

CAPTAIN FLINDERS

Shortly after the *Polyphemus* docked in England, John Franklin was traveling in a post chaise up the road from London. The horses snorted and paced their way briskly along the road that skirted the fens south of Spilsby. His heart warmed to the sight of the familiar church with its square tower and pinnacles silhouetted against the sky.

The carriage stopped beside the market house, near the center of town. Opposite stood the Franklin home, where John had been born in 1786. He stepped out and drew himself up straight-backed in a pose befitting his midshipman's uniform. Swiftly he placed in position the big cocked hat and the dirk, or short sword, and walked to the house.

What a reception he must have received! No doubt his sisters Sarah, Hannah, Isabella, and Henrietta burst through the door and showered him with questions. When he got inside, his parents and his brothers, Willingham and James, must have embraced him warmly.

Then the Battle of Copenhagen was doubtless refought in the Franklin household, with lavish descriptions of the tricky shoals and passages, of Nelson's fleet in trouble, of Sir Hyde signaling to retreat, of Nelson putting a telescope to his blind eye and going ahead . . . We can well imagine that the stories were delivered to the delight of all.

But then came the question on all their minds: where next?

"Where next" was to be an answer to young John's wildest hopes and dreams. We do not know from whom he first received the news, but since his new commander-to-be was actually a cousin, he may have been informed by his father. And if that is true, the conversation might have gone something like this:

"My boy, I've news for you."

"You've heard from Flinders?"

"Not so quickly! Yes, I have heard from him."

"What does he say? Am I to go with him?"

"God knows why my youngest son must be taken from me for a sailor's life. John, you've always been sensible—"

"Please, Father, if I'm to go with Captain Flinders . . ."

"As if it weren't enough for Thomas to be in the cavalry and James about to join the East India Company . . . Why can't you enroll at Oxford, like Willingham, lest all my sons fly away?"

"Father—"

"Well, I may as well nail my plea to the masthead. This passion for seafaring has filled your bones. God go with you on the *Investigator*."

"It's true! When does she leave? Quickly, eh?"

"You've time enough, my son, to enjoy another day in Spilsby. It will be a hard trip. This business will take you to the far side of the earth."

"I know that perfectly, sir."

"But Terra Australis—do you know what it is like?"

"I can tell you, sir—"

"Can you tell me of the savages, the naked savages who threatened Captain Cook? Can you tell me of the settlements? Ah, yes, you say, there is Port Jackson. But what is so little a village in so wild a land?"

"You think that I fear it, sir?"

"I know you don't, my boy. But you'll need every ounce of patience and bravery you've got. Captain Flinders is a good seaman. He's young—only twenty-seven—but voyages with Bass and Bligh have seasoned him. He's been in battle and twice to the other side of the earth. He knows Australia as no other. Were it not for that, I would have found you another vessel . . . or none at all."

John Franklin counted the moments until he got to Spithead, a seaport on the southern shore of England. He made his way to the wharves and there, for the first time, set eyes upon the ship that was to carry him south into the unknown.

Any young sailor would have been proud of the *Investigator*. She was a 334-ton sloop, built in the north of England for the merchant service. Now she rode silently at anchor, her sails furled and braced. Soon those sails would drop, the anchor would be raised, and . . .

John climbed aboard and made his way to the captain's cabin.

"John Franklin, my dear cousin," said the captain, rising and coming forward to shake hands. Flinders' eyes were large and friendly, his forehead wide and low, his mouth small. The high collar of his commander's uniform gave him a stiffly erect appearance. The golden epaulets on his shoulders and rows of buttons down each side of his chest gave him an air of authority. "How I have been waiting to see you again. Do tell me about

Spilsby. I miss Lincolnshire, especially at this season. Sit down. Now, how is your family?"

John had not known Flinders well, having seen him but a few times and those when he was much younger. In a rush, the tales of Flinders' exploits came swimming into John's head. Flinders had sailed under Captain William Bligh to Tahiti, near where the famous mutiny of the crew of Bligh's ship *Bounty* had taken place years earlier. Bligh had liked Flinders. So had the Admiralty.

On his next trip to Terra Australis, Flinders had set out from Port Jackson with famed explorer George Bass, in a tiny ship called the *Tom Thumb*. This vessel measured eight feet long and five feet wide, scarcely big enough for the two of them; yet in it they explored a number of rivers and bays. They were upset and dumped ashore, guided by Indians, pushed and pulled in heavy storms, and mauled by giant waves and violent seas.

All Europe had been amazed at what these young explorers had done—all in a land with scarcely a single European and on the far side of the earth.

"My family send their regards, sir," John said, taking a chair beside the captain's desk. "They wish you well."

"Your worthy father, I trust, has informed you of the nature of this voyage?"

"Yes, sir."

Captain Flinders drew a leather pouch from his desk and took some papers from it. "Our orders are just received. We shall be leaving soon."

"For New Holland, sir?" the boy asked.

Flinders put down his papers and looked up. "Some call it New Holland," he said. "Some call it Terra Australis. I call it Australia, a term more agreeable to the ear."

Captain Flinders (from a print, 1814)

"Australia, then, sir . . ."

"Yes. We are ordered to survey the coast, to discover such harbors as there may be, and to investigate any opening likely to lead to a strait or an inland sea. We are to keep a journal of the winds and weather, the fertility of the soil, the manners and customs of the inhabitants . . ."

"The Indians, sir? Are they not unfriendly? I have read the journals of Captain Cook."

Flinders smiled. "Let us see if we can find some friendly ones! Now, Franklin, the Admiralty instructions which will be of most concern to you are these: You will fix the true positions both in latitude and longitude of headlands, bays, and harbors by astronomical observations. You will note the variation of the compass needle and the direction and course of tides and currents."

"Have we the instruments, sir?"

Flinders rose and motioned John to a cabinet behind the desk. Opening it, he said: "There you are, my boy. Timekeepers, watches, chronometers, theodolites, sextants, a reflecting circle. And this is an Arnold's watch to take with us when we go in the small boats up rivers into the interior."

John's eyes were wide. "We are going inland, sir?"

"Oho, yes, by gar!" Flinders closed the cabinet. "Our orders require us to explore wherever I think prudent." Returning to the desk, he picked up the orders again. "We are to examine Torres Strait, the Gulf of Carpentaria, then the north and west coasts of Australia."

Marine timekeeper by Larcum Kendall, completed 1769

"You mean we are to circumnavigate the continent?"

"If it be an island, yes."

"That has not been done before, Captain."

"Correct, my boy."

"But what of the French, sir? We are at war."

Flinders sighed as if a trifle vexed. "We are awaiting a passport from the French. I think Napoleon will grant us the courtesies we grant vessels of exploration in time of war. After all, French exploring ships even now sail the high seas for Australia."

The captain rose and went to the door. "It will be a hard voyage, and a dangerous one. His Majesty expects every man to do his utmost."

The dock was soon a lively place, with rattling wagons and falling boxes, with sailors singing as they repaired the sails and tested the rigging, and with quartermasters shouting to workmen who hauled in supplies of every description. Aboard and below went stores of bread, salt pork, and water. Loaded and locked in the hold were gifts for the Indians.

"Five hundred pocket knives," shouted the clerk. "Five hundred looking glasses . . . 100 combs . . . 200 strings of beads . . . 100 pairs of earrings . . . 200 finger rings . . . one thousand yards of blue and red cloth . . . 100 red caps . . . one thousand needles . . . 300 pairs of scissors . . . 100 hammers . . . 50 axes . . . 200 hatchets . . . Ah, here's a bundle of medals and coins."

John could hardly believe that they would use all these—there weren't that many Indians in Australia! But then he remembered that the *Investigator* was being fitted for a voyage of three full years.

As he met the crew, he quickly learned that the men of an exploring ship were different from those of a man-of-war such as the *Polyphemus*. Here were an astronomer, a naturalist, and a painter to record the wild things that lived or grew in Australia. There were a gardener and a miner, too.

He met them all in those last days ashore. There was Lieutenant Fowler and the Master, John Thistle. The

tween the planks were filled with a fibrous tarred material called oakum. Seamen shifted the top masts, inspected the rigging, and took on water, wine, and beef.

Four days later the *Investigator* sailed again. The winds now were variable, sometimes puffing out the sails, sometimes dying away so that the sails would hang and flap in idle breezes. When the wind did blow, it came from nearly every quarter of the compass, and frequently with rain.

Not long after Madeira, the carpenter reported to the captain: "The oakum is working out of the seams again, sir."

"By gad, my lads," Flinders exclaimed, "this is the devil! The ship is destined to encounter every hazard, and already she is leaking."

"Can't we get another ship at the Cape of Good Hope, sir?" John asked.

"We are at war," Flinders answered. "I was given to understand that no better ship could be spared from the service. My ambition was—and is—to make such a minute investigation of Australia that no person shall have occasion to come after us to make further discoveries. It must be done with the ship we have, and God help us. Had I refused to accept this vessel we should still be ashore in England."

As they crossed the Equator—with appropriate ceremony and merriment—fresh winds and frequent squalls blew around the ship. The swell from the south caused the ship to strain its seams and timbers, so Flinders altered course to sail upon the beam. To keep the ship from being topheavy, carronades and supplies were taken off the decks and stored in the hold.

Three adult and three young Gannets on nest

"After this was done," Flinders wrote in his journal, "the tremulous motion caused by every blow of the sea, exciting a sensation as if the ship were elastic, was considerably diminished; and the quantity of water admitted by the leaks was also somewhat reduced."

Each day they saw a multitude of birds, including gannets, shearwaters, pintados, and sooty petrels. Man-o-war birds circled high overhead. Once a swallow stayed with the ship for several days, darting past the ports and lee scuttles.

The standing orders of the *Investigator* were that on every clear day the deck below and the officers' quarters were to be thoroughly cleaned, washed, and aired. They were then to be dried with the help of fires in stoves, and finally sprinkled with vinegar. Flinders felt so strongly about maintaining the good health of his men that he had long ago determined to follow the ship procedures first practiced by Captain Cook.

Even when it was wet or the sky overcast, the decks were cleaned and aired. Every two or three weeks, as circumstances permitted, each man spread out on deck and exposed to sun and air the contents of his sea-chest or bag and the whole of his bedding. Flinders gave orders that no man was ever to sleep on deck or lie down when his clothes were wet.

Each Sunday and Thursday morning, the ship's company was mustered, and every man appeared clean-shaven and neatly dressed. "When the evenings were fine," Flinders recorded, "the drum and fife announced the forecastle to be the scene of dancing; nor did I discourage other playful amusements which might occasionally be more to the taste of the sailors, and were not unseasonable."

The greatest scourge of the times was scurvy, a dread disease in which the flesh became soft, the legs and gums swelled painfully, and the teeth began to loosen in their sockets. As Flinders well knew, a man with scurvy was useless on a voyage. Worse yet, he had to be tended by others. Consequently, they all drank lime juice as an antiscorbutic in the Tropics, and ate sauerkraut in cooler climates.

Man O'War birds

Apart from this, Flinders knew how to keep his men well fed. The cook boiled oatmeal for breakfast four days in the week. At other times a portable broth, in cakes, was served along with onions, pepper, and other seasonings that added pleasantly to the regular diet of salt meat. Lunch each day consisted of a biscuit eaten with wort, a fermented drink made by pouring boiling water on the essence of malt.

Never did Flinders restrict his men in the use of fresh water. Though care was taken to keep from wasting it, each man drank what he wished, and took as much as he needed for washing.

So well did these procedures work, and so well was discipline kept that Flinders enjoyed the satisfaction of seeing, as he put it, "my people orderly and full of zeal for the service in which we were engaged."

Because of this zeal, they did not remain long at the Cape of Good Hope, on the southern tip of Africa. A gang of caulkers came aboard the *Investigator* from other British ships that lay anchored there and thoroughly caulked her seams, inside and out. The botanists, who explored Table Mountain and other nearby features collecting plants, were loath to leave when the time for departure came.

But Flinders had every intention of taking advantage of the approaching summer. It was now November 4, and spring had begun. So once again the anchor was raised, the sails unfurled, and the little exploring ship steered eastward into the vastness of the Indian Ocean.

The winds were steadily fair and westerly, and the *Investigator* sometimes traveled more than 150 miles a day. For Midshipman Franklin it was the thrill of his young lifetime. Day and night he made observations of the sky, the sea, and the weather. He took the temperature and specific gravity, or weight, of sea water at various depths by bringing up samples in specially constructed buckets.

As the weeks slipped by, he learned that navigation was not a simple science. Men still knew little about it. "Navigation," said one of the books in the ship's library, "is that art whereby we are enabled to conduct, or carry a ship, from one port to another. This science depends upon some parts of the mathematics, which must be known before we can treat of it; therefore we shall first lay down the principles of *Geometry*."

Straightaway he plunged into a study of angles and triangles, of formulas for measuring lines and arcs that were known, and formulas for measuring those unknown. He swiftly discovered that finding angles on paper helped him to determine angles between the earth and sun and thereby calculate the ship's position.

"Can you give me the logarithm of 342?" the captain asked one day.

John quickly thumbed through a book of tables. "Here it is, sir."

"Good boy. You're doing well with Mr. Harris."

He was speaking of Joseph Harris's manual, *A Treatise of Navigation*. John knew it well. Navigation, it said, was simply conducting a ship in the fastest way and the shortest time between two places. "When the places proposed are at no great distance, but so that a ship may sail in sight of land, or within soundings, it is then called *Coasting* . . ."

John knew that coasting was about the only way the early Greeks had been able to sail from place to place. They had had no compasses. They dared not get out of sight of land. How could they know of the rest of the world? They couldn't sail across the ocean without familiar landmarks.

This being the case, John wondered how Ferdinand Magellan had managed to circumnavigate the world so long ago. Of course, by 1519 a few crude navigational devices had been invented and Magellan had them: a globe built a few years before, a map of the world by Leonardo da Vinci, wood and metal theodolites—instruments for measuring angles on the horizon, quadrants, compasses, magnetic needles, hour glasses, and rudimentary timepieces.

"The proper business of navigation," Harris went on, "is how to conduct a ship through the wide and pathless ocean, where nothing is visible but sky and water for a considerable time . . ."

Smoothly through the southern sea rode the *Investigator,* aimed for what destiny not even John could imagine. After the caulking she had gotten at the Cape of Good Hope, she no longer leaked as she had. But the question in the mind of every man was: would it last?

From time to time the spouting of whales could be seen off the bows of the vessels. At other times the ship shook to its core as the big guns blasted away in firing tests. Occasionally the marines practiced shooting with their rifles.

John stood frequently at the binnacle, or compass stand, looking out across the ocean. "The wide and pathless ocean," Harris had called it. How true, John thought. It had no paths, no roads, no village spires by which the traveler might be guided. The mariner had only the celestial objects—the sun, the moon, the stars.

John tried in vain to hold the sextant steady, to keep the horizon level in his viewing tube—but it was no use. The ship so often pitched and rolled with the swell or the wind that steady and careful observations at sea were nearly impossible.

"For finding the place of the ship at any time," said Harris, "and consequently the bearing and distance of the place intended for, the mariner has these helps: viz., the course steered . . ."

Yes, John knew that. He had plotted daily the ship's actual direction of sailing.

". . . the distance sailed . . ." Well, you could not keep an accurate check of distance covered on that pathless ocean.

". . . the latitude by observation; which last indeed is the only certain data mariners (at present) have at sea . . ."

He found and recorded the latitude daily, by measuring angles between the celestial objects and the earth. Day and night he worked and studied. By oil lamp he pored over charts and memorized tables of figures.

They soon began to notice seaweed alongside the ship. New birds flew over. The color of the water changed. In his eagerness for sight of land, John must have stood on tiptoe on the quarterdeck or even climbed the rigging to make out the uneven horizon of the strange, new country whose shores they were about to see.

On December 6, 1801, the voices of the lookouts loudly rang in the breeze: "Land ho! Land ho on the larboard!"

Almost immediately there was a pounding of feet and excited shouting of voices. Men clattered on deck and lined the railing and rigging and bulwarks.

Four

AUSTRALIA

Anxiously they watched as the land came into view— a sloping, rocky coast, lightly covered with trees and shrubs, with islets scattered on the south side of a cape.

Already Westall, the artist, was sketching the scene. John was silent, his gaze ranging first over the near hills, then to the tops of higher ones inland. He saw no Indians, no huts, no fires or smoke.

Returning to the binnacle, John found Flinders reading from the azimuth scale, a circle divided into 360 equal arcs, or degrees. By sighting across this, or "taking an azimuth," Flinders could determine the direction of the land as it lay from the ship. Each time he got a bearing this way, he jotted the number of degrees in his journal. Thus was recorded the position of major capes and bays and headlands.

No one is quite sure who the first person to see Australia was. As far back as the thirteenth century, there seems to have been a tradition about the existence of a great and unknown southern land.

The Spanish explorer, De Torres, approached it closely in 1606, and may have actually seen the Australian coast. That same year, the first Europeans landed—the Dutch. They named some of the landmarks, explored a

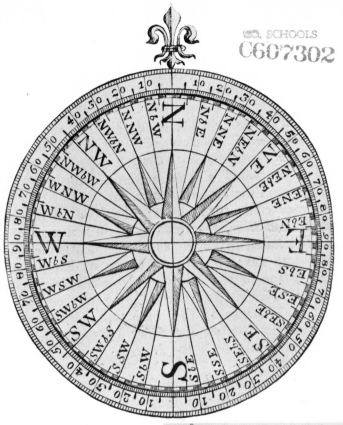

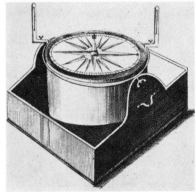

Above: Azimuth circle, containing not only the 360 degrees (divided into quadrants of 90 degrees), but also the cardinal points. *Right:* Azimuth compass.

while, and wrote the first account of the kangaroo. By 1665 the Dutch had made some maps of parts of the coast and named the land New Holland.

Dutch captains bound for Java and other ports in the spice trade sailed past various parts of the coast and gave them different names. Then came the voyages in 1643 and 1644 of Abel Tasman, who had been directed to find out what the southern portion of the world was like, "whether it be land or sea, or icebergs, whatever God has ordained to be there." During this period the English buccaneer William Dampier visited places along the western coast.

That was only the beginning. Captain Cook on his voyage of 1770 explored the entire east coast and gave the world more information than had been obtained from all prior voyages combined. He called the country New South Wales.

In 1791, ten years before the present voyage, George Vancouver sighted the southwestern corner of Australia and discovered King George's Sound. (For places mentioned in this chapter, see map, page 44.) But adverse winds had borne down on Vancouver and so he resumed his voyage across the Pacific to the northwest coast of North America.

That was all that was known in Flinders' time. Some geographers thought that the land might be divided into two huge islands, because of the known existence of a large embayment on the northern coast. That gulf or strait, or whatever it was (it had been named the Gulf of Carpentaria), still lay unmapped. From there to the south stretched a vast blank area unknown and unexplored. And nearly the whole south coast had never been explored.

Even Bass Strait, despite what Bass and Flinders had been able to discover, still remained a mystery; the question of a strait between Australia and Van Diemen's Land was still not settled.

Each day the ship sailed eastward, along the southern coast, as close to shore as safety allowed. Flinders drew on his charts or perched at the masthead scanning the coastlands with a telescope. Seamen repeatedly hurled into the water heavy weights to which they had securely fastened ropes. These weights they allowed to sink to the bottom, then hauled them up to determine the depth of the sea near shore.

By now, the *Investigator* needed repairs again, so they watched for a sheltered bay and finally moored in one called Princess-Royal Harbor. The captain went ashore with the naturalists and selected a place to erect the tents in which surveying and nautical instruments would be placed. After that, he ascended the highest hill to take some angles.

The ship's topmasts were struck and repairs begun. The naturalists and artists ranged in all directions ashore, and everyone was on orders to keep a lookout for birds and mammals, plants and insects. From time to time, other members of the crew went ashore for relaxation.

With no time to spare, Flinders rapidly moved between the observatory—where Franklin and the officers were making observations—and other points from which measurements could be taken. Here on shore the motion of the ship was not a problem and once again the instruments could be accurately read. From the headlands and other vantage points, the captain, with his theodolites and signal flags, directed some of his men in smaller boats as they moved around the harbor taking soundings.

On the 14th of December, they saw on the horizon smoke from distant campfires. At once a party set out toward it and, for the first time, met several of the natives.

The Australians were dark, broad-shouldered men with large mouths and long teeth. They wore no clothes whatever, although some had a cloak of kangaroo skin thrown over the shoulders. Judging from their actions and appearance they were hunters rather than fishermen. Their manner was quick and brusque, their talking rapid and sometimes loud. The language sounded as if it would be difficult to imitate, but Flinders listed some of the words for later comparison with other Indian languages and with lists of words compiled by previous navigators.

Determined to make all signs of friendship to the people he met, Flinders gave them a bird that had recently been shot, and a handkerchief, but these did not produce the desired effect. Instead, the Indians indicated that they wanted the Englishmen to return to their ship and go away.

The next morning, other natives appeared on the hill behind the tents. At first they came up cautiously, spears upraised, shouting words that seemed to mean, "Go away! Go away!"

The assistant surgeon gave them toys and articles of iron, receiving some of their crude implements in exchange. For the moment, peace was sustained, but the English later found their mirrors and other presents lying along the shore, so the giving of gifts was discontinued.

The following week a well-armed party of thirteen— led by Flinders—set off to examine the lakes behind West Cape Howe. On the way they encountered several Indians, and were once again warned to go away.

Flinders and his party made their way through swamps and through thick woods of eucalyptus trees. Despite the apparent barrenness of the land, there was a great deal for Robert Brown, the naturalist, to observe and collect. As usual, Ferdinand Bauer, the painter of natural history, and William Westall, the painter of landscapes, were busily sketching what they saw—eucalyptus and casuarina trees, pitcher plants, lizards, kangaroos, cassowaries, lakes, rivers, and views of the sea.

In the meantime, wood and water had been collected and stowed aboard the *Investigator*. Sails had been repaired and rigging refitted. The day for departure arrived.

"Our friends, the natives, continued to visit us," Flinders wrote in his journal, "and the old man, with several others being at the tents this morning, I ordered the party of marines on shore, to be exercised in their presence.

"The red coats and white crossed belts [of the marines] were greatly admired, having some resemblance to their own manner of ornamenting themselves; and the drum, but particularly the fife, excited their astonishment; but when they saw these beautiful red-and-white men, with their bright muskets, drawn up in a line, they absolutely screamed with delight; nor were their wild gestures and vociferation to be silenced, but by commencing the exercise, to which they paid the most earnest and silent attention.

"Several of [the Indians] moved their hands, involuntarily, according to the motions; and the old man placed himself at the end of the rank, with a short staff in his hand, which he shouldered, presented, grounded, as did the marines their muskets, without, I believe, knowing what he did.

"Before firing, the Indians were made acquainted with what was going to take place; so that the vollies did not excite much terror."

The coming of the new year, 1802, found them coasting eastward again. As usual, Flinders tried to keep as close as possible to the coast and often remained for hours at the masthead, surveying the land with his telescope.

Compass bearings taken and recorded by day were checked at night. The captain plotted progress charts and brought his journal of observations, bearings, and remarks to date.

Franklin all the time was watching, listening, working, measuring, and studying.

They still could not explain those constant vexing variations in compass readings. They took azimuths from the binnacle—where the compass ordinarily rested. Then, with the same compass, they took azimuths from the other end of the ship. The readings were different by three degrees. To vessels whose very survival depended on finding directions accurately, this was serious. Something was affecting the compass. Could it be the iron used in building the ship?

The wind now shifted to the east and blew against them steadily. For days at a time they beat to windward, making little progress. Close watch was kept on the barometer, whose pressure readings told them when to brace for lowering weather.

Although the horizon was hazy and hard to see, Flinders recorded the coastline almost rock by rock in his journal: breakers, islets, archipelagoes, beaches, ridges, bottoms, capes, and bights.

Still bothered by the compass variations, he took his instruments ashore one day and checked them carefully, only to discover that the needles were affected by the rocks themselves! Wherever there was granite or basalt, or wherever the rocks contained fair amounts of iron, the compass readings were affected. On limestone and sandstone—rocks containing smaller amounts of iron—he noted fewer variations.

League after league they sailed along the shore of the Great Australian Bight. Exploring here and there, the vessel followed an erratic track. As the days passed by, the ship tacked and wore, stretched away, braced up, worked out, ran in, stood off, and went through what must have seemed a thousand different maneuvers.

Now and then a party was sent ashore at dusk to hunt for petrels. It wasn't always easy. At times they found few birds, and even the fish were scarce. As January passed, the summer heat became intense. Once, when he climbed a cliff, Flinders estimated the temperature to be 120 degrees.

Continuing his discoveries, the captain named geographic features in honor of family, friends, and members of the Admiralty. He also honored his officers and crewmen, which accounted for such place names as Fowler's Bay, Point Brown, Cape Bauer, Point Westall, and Franklin's Isles. For the Lincolnshire men, he bestowed the names of Port Lincoln, Louth Bay, and Spilsby Isle.

Around the Great Bight they noted suspicious changes in the tide and, to the excitement of all, the discovery of a great gulf was predicted. Sure enough, they soon sailed into a large bay and named it Spencer Gulf. Perhaps here they would discover whether the continent was cut in half, and whether this gulf connected with the gulf on the northern coast.

At dusk one evening the cutter, with the master, a midshipman, and six sailors aboard, was seen under sail returning to the *Investigator* from the mainland when suddenly it seemed to vanish. Lieutenant Fowler went out in a boat and searched by lantern for two hours without success. He fired a gun. No answer. Returning in the dark, the lieutenant himself narrowly escaped being over-turned in the rippling tide.

Muskets were fired from the ship. Shouts were kept up. All through the night the men maintained a vigil. Next day they steered toward the mainland and sent a boat ashore to search. Presently they found the cutter dashed and broken against the rocks.

The eight men were never found. Sadly, Flinders named the nearest headland Cape Catastrophe.

The more they explored in Spencer Gulf the more they saw that nothing in the way of a strait divided the land. Australia might well be a single island. It seemed a well-inhabited one, for smoke and fires were often seen along the shores and inland. Flinders and his men discovered primitive huts and heaps of oyster shells. One night they heard the howling of dogs.

Leaving Spencer Gulf they landed on an island inhabited chiefly by kangaroos. These animals provided the first real feast of fresh meat the men of the expedition had had in months, and the gunners shot enough to provide a delicious meal for everyone. Thenceforth, the place was known as Kangaroo Island.

April came. As summer faded, the days grew shorter and cooler. The hint of coming winter, with its sweeping coastal gales, could be felt in the air. These signs compelled the captain to move on, though he would have liked to stay a longer time on Kangaroo Island.

Late on the afternoon of April 8, the lookout cried: "White rock ahead!"

As they sailed closer they could see that it was not a rock but a sail! The excitement of seeing their first ship since leaving Africa may well be imagined. But excitement turned to anxiety. As they drew nearer, a single question burned in each man's mind. Was it friendly—or was it French?

"Clear the decks for action!" the lieutenant called. The *Investigator* burst into hurried activity. Flinders sent up the Union Jack (which had just been adopted the year before as the British flag). The oncoming ship ran up the French tricolor.

Kangaroo Island. An engraving made from William Westall's original painting, showing the heavy vegetation and rocky character of the island. Seals lounge on the shore at left, and kangaroos in the right foreground. Two emus (now the National Bird of Australia) can be seen beneath the large tree

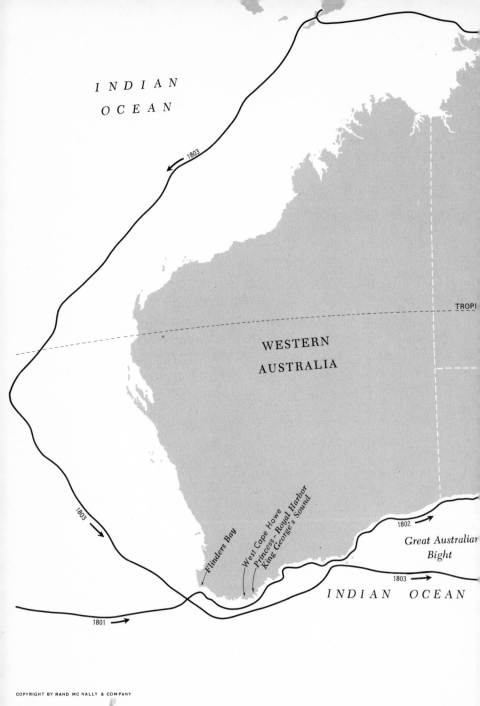

INDIAN
OCEAN

1803

WESTERN

AUSTRALIA

TROPI

INDIAN   OCEAN

Great Australiar
Bight

1802

1803

1803

Flinders Bay

West Cape Howe
Princess - Royal Harbor
King George's Sound

1801

Australia, showing places mentioned in Chapters 4 and 5; also route
of H. M. S. *Investigator,* on the first circumnavigation of Australia,

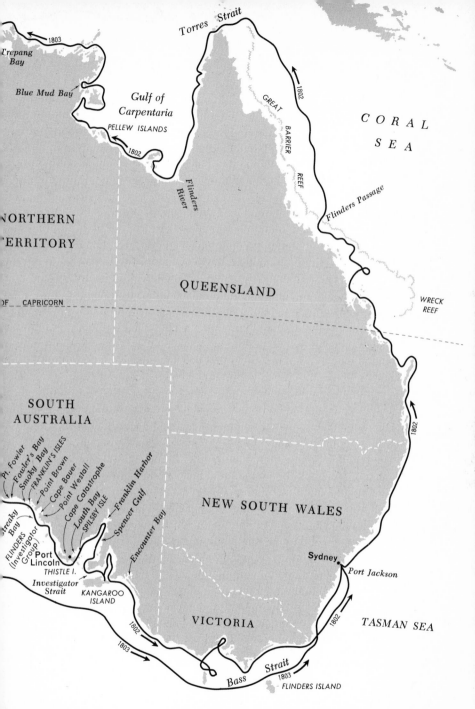

...tarting from Cape of Good Hope, December 1801, as shown on Flinders' charts in the Atlas to his *Voyage* to Terra Australis, 1814.

Five

AROUND
THE CONTINENT

It was the *Géographe*, the French exploring ship
When the two vessels drew abreast of each other and
hove to under a flag of truce, Flinders went aboard the
Géographe.

Not until after dark did he return. The officers listened
intently as he spoke. "Captain Baudin tells me that the
Géographe and her companion ship were separated in a
violent storm a month ago, east of us, near the entrance
to Bass Strait. Baudin sailed on through the strait, and
has followed the coast northwesterly to this point.

"It is a pitiful state of affairs over there, my lads. The
ship's meat is spoiled and filled with worms. The crew is
racked with scurvy and other diseases."

Early next morning Baudin and Flinders met again
and traded information about the tides and winds and
ocean currents. Then the encounter (which was respon-
sible for the name Encounter Bay) was over.

John Franklin watched the sails of the *Géographe*
disappear to the west. On the other side of the world the
French and English were spilling blood in battle. He
wondered how the war was going. Sometimes he thought
of his family, and of the moors and fens of Lincolnshire.

Steady winds held back the ship as she sailed to the
east. Spray filled the sky and blurred the land; so high

were the waves and so dangerous the winds that Flinders dared not approach the coast. They swung through Bass Strait, charting as best they could, and on up the eastern coast to Port Jackson. Here, in one of the finest ports in the world, with its wide, natural harbor, lay the colony of Sydney, a small collection of huts and buildings.

The *Investigator* moved in to anchor among the other vessels—a brig, a whaler, a privateer, an armed ship, and Captain Baudin's companion ship, the French *Naturaliste*.

Flinders felt a great sense of pride at the complete success of his voyage so far. "There was not a single individual on board who was not on deck working the ship into harbour," he wrote, "and it may be averred that the officers and crew were, generally speaking, in better health than on the day we sailed from Spithead, and not in less good spirits."

Immediately upon disembarking, Franklin and others set up tents and astronomical instruments and established an observatory ashore. Flinders called upon the Governor and related to him the events of the voyage and the discoveries that had been made.

The twelve weeks they stayed in Sydney were busy weeks, and Port Jackson hummed with preparations for continuance of the *Investigator's* voyage. The ship's masts were stripped and rerigged, stores examined, and new supplies loaded aboard. A boat was made to replace the lost cutter, and the brig *Lady Nelson* was placed under Flinders' command to help in furthering the explorations. The naturalist and painters went on trips inland, examining the countryside and studying its wildlife and plants. Flinders made charts of his discoveries for the Admiralty.

Remote as it was, this colony enjoyed a spirited social life. News had arrived that France and England were at

An engraving by William Westall of Port Jackson, as it looked when the *Investigator* was there. The colony of Sydney can be seen in the distance, near the ships anchored in the harbor

peace again, so Flinders and the Frenchmen dined together and traded information freely. There were celebrations of holidays. There were dinners. There were balls. Flinders invited officers of other vessels to dine on the *Investigator,* and when they came, he and his crewmen greeted them with salutes and ceremonies.

Dull and rainy weather made celestial observations difficult or impossible at the observatory. By seizing the opportunities that did arrive, however, they obtained sufficient data to determine the rates of timekeepers and "to answer the purposes of geography and navigation."

John Franklin assisted in taking thirty meridian altitudes so as to determine precisely the latitude of Port Jackson, and helped to draw up forty-four sets of distances of the sun and moon from which to determine the longitude.

One of the most useful instruments in the determination of longitude was the chronometer, a timepiece that had to be absolutely accurate. The chronometer (which means time-measurer) had been invented in 1735, not long before John's day, but its value had not been fully demonstrated until about 1775.

After that, the precise time could be maintained on all ships at sea and the longitude could be found by relatively simple calculations based on the elapsed time of travel. Flinders carried aboard the *Investigator* a famous chronometer known as the Kendall and Mudge K3. It had been used on the third and final voyage of Captain Cook, and then had helped to guide Vancouver. It was a good instrument. Indeed, the chronometers of a century later were little different from those of Flinders' day.

The icy, wintry winds of July made Flinders anxious to be on the way again. Accordingly, on July 21, 1802, the *Investigator,* accompanied by the brig *Lady Nelson,* sailed from Sydney and headed north.

As they glided swiftly through the Tasman Sea, the air grew warmer. Soon they entered the Coral Sea and approached a series of coral ridges known as the Great Barrier Reef. Although these ridges enclosed magnificent stretches of emerald water, they were dangerous to ships. Captain Cook had nearly been wrecked in passing among them, and Flinders wanted to find a channel. After several tries, he did—the route today is known as Flinders Passage—and went on to anchor in Torres Strait on October

29. The little brig had not been able to keep up with the *Investigator,* so Flinders had sent her back to Port Jackson ten days before.

Three long Papuan canoes, bearing about fifty native islanders, hove into view. Flinders braced the ship for an attack. But these were friendly natives and he presented them with a handsaw, a hammer, nails, and other trifles and continued his voyage.

The time had now come to enter the Gulf of Carpentaria. The captain was elated. At last they could determine the nature of the gulf and examine any openings into the interior.

They landed first on the eastern shore, after having found a place to careen the ship, or tip her partly on her side so as to clean and caulk the bottom. When the carpenters examined the timbers, some were found to be rotten. They dug out whole handfuls of decaying wood. All this obviously meant that the old ship was weaker than anyone had supposed. In a strong gale, with much sea running, she would surely founder.

When their examination was finished, the carpenters announced their assessment of the *Investigator:* totally unfit for bad weather. Furthermore, they said, she had only twelve months more of sailing. After that, there wouldn't be a sound timber in her.

John relayed this information to the captain, and it must have been a heartbreaking experience for them both.

"I have endeavored," Flinders said, "to follow the land so closely as to see the washing of the surf upon it. We have missed no opening, no headland, nothing. Now, with a ship unable to stand a storm . . ."

The next step was obvious. They must return to Port Jackson. But because of contrary monsoon winds, they could not return the way they had come. Besides, getting through the barrier reef again was too hazardous with a rotten ship.

Flinders decided to see what they could of the gulf in which they now were located, then to sail westerly and around the other side of Australia.

As the expedition continued, they found a number of rivers entering the gulf—one of which is now called Flinders River—but no major strait or channel leading into the heart of the continent. They explored a group of islands named after Sir Edward Pellew, a heroic naval officer. After that, disaster struck. In Blue Mud Bay, the master's mate was killed by a native's spear and one of the English seamen shot another native in retaliation.

Flinders exploded when he heard the news. "That's just the kind of bloodshed I did *not* want. This is a peaceful voyage!"

For nearly three months they examined and mapped the Gulf of Carpentaria and on February 17, 1803, sailed out of it and west along the Australian coast.

Before long, six Malayan vessels were met, and from the chief of one they learned that sixty ships were coming from Macassar to hunt for *beche-de-mer.* This is a kind of sea animal, also called *trepang,* or sea cucumber, that occurs in great numbers off the northern Australian coast. When collected, it was boiled, dried, smoked, and shipped to China where it was esteemed in the making of soup.

The months slipped by, and on board ship conditions worsened. Food ran low, and what they gathered ashore was not very nourishing. Mosquitoes, flies, the hot and humid climate—all had bad effects upon the crew. Scurvy began, the disease that any captain dreaded. Flinders

A scene in Sir Edward Pellew's Group (engraving made from an original painting by William Westall)

himself developed ulcers on his feet, so severe that he could no longer stand in his favorite place at the masthead.

About the only healthy passenger, it seemed, was Trim, the cat, and his good spirits raised those of the men a little.

Straightaway they sailed, week after week. To Franklin, working daily with the sextants and chronometers, it was disappointing not to go on trips inland or to map the coast as carefully as they had done before. Down the western coast they sailed, then under the continent, across the Great Australian Bight, and past familiar Kangaroo Island.

Dysentery broke out and became so bad that six men

died from it. When finally they sailed into the harbor of Port Jackson and anchored at Sydney on June 9, 1803, the crew was far less healthy than when it had left there nearly a year before. But they were heroes. For the first time in history, the Australian continent had been circumnavigated. Their mission for the Admiralty had been carried out.

Captain Flinders, however, did not bask long in glory. He consulted with the Governor about further surveys of Australia, and began to lay his plans. He would need a new ship now, and new supplies. The place to get those was in England, so he decided to leave for home and lay his charts and proposals before the Admiralty.

Within a month the captain and twenty-one others from the *Investigator,* including Midshipman Franklin, embarked as passengers for England aboard the *Porpoise,* a small armed ship. This vessel, together with the *Cato,* of London, and the *Bridgewater,* a craft belonging to the East India Company, sailed out of Port Jackson on the 10th of July and steered northwesterly.

For five weeks the voyage was uneventful. Then calamity struck. On the night of August 17, the vessels sailed quietly through the darkness. It was cloudy, with a fresh breeze blowing. John walked on deck for a while, chatting with the warrant officer on the forecastle. They watched the dim silhouettes and the lights of the *Cato,* a mile away on the larboard quarter, and the *Bridgewater,* half a mile to starboard. At eight o'clock he watched the soundings being taken and listened for the reading.

"No bottom at 35 fathoms, sir."

All being well, he went below. He had gotten as far as the lower deck when a frantic shout came from above and was repeated throughout the ship.

"Breakers ahead! Breakers ahead!"

Instantly the ship was in bedlam. Men leaped from their hammocks. Feet pounded on the stairs and Franklin joined the frantic rush on deck. Passengers scurried everywhere, some of them still in their undershirts or with bare feet. High overhead, crewmen desperately tried to shorten sail and bring the ship around.

"Haul out the mizzen-staysail! Hurry!"

"Look alive, you impudent dogs! Move!"

Everyone by now was shouting. John rushed to the railing. Instantly he froze. Waves were crashing on rocks not three ships' lengths ahead.

"The current's got us!"

"We're going to hit!"

"God preserve us!"

John reached for the railing to brace himself. All at once the ship struck with a crash and rending of wood. Splinters and beams flew in all directions.

"Get down! Get down!"

"She's heeling over!"

John was thrown from his feet, as were others, in the lurching ship. Heavy spray hit him as he tried to rise. Grasping a stanchion, he pulled himself to his feet just as another crash was heard. The ship jolted sharply. He looked up just in time to see the foremast crack and topple over the side.

"We're done for!" someone shouted.

John pulled himself to the rail and looked down. It was a fearful sight, nearly invisible in the darkness. White surf surged against and over the ship, carrying with it whole chunks of the *Porpoise* that had been ripped loose. The ship had rammed into a coral reef.

Six

WRECK REEF

As she crashed and splintered again and again, the *Porpoise* heeled over toward the reef, so that the spray flew over her but did not fill her. Helplessly the men aboard clung to the stricken ship and watched the companion vessel *Cato* come up, her crewmen trying desperately to shift her course. It was too late.

"In a few minutes," Flinder wrote, the *Cato* "struck the reef about two cables length from us. We saw her fall over on her broad side, and the masts almost instantly disappeared . . . By heeling over to windward, she presented her unsheltered decks to the sea, which broke in upon them in a most furious manner, tearing them up, and everything within the ship, almost in an instant; and the crew had no place left where they could shelter themselves from the seas, but in the larboard fore chains, where they were all crowded together, the greater part naked.

"The *Cato* had hung up on a rock nearly in the middle, and every time the sea struck her, she twisted about with such violent jerks that they expected the stern, which was down in the water, would part every moment . . ."

In this double disaster, Flinders decided immediately to go out to the *Bridgewater,* which somehow had missed the reef and was still afloat. Speed was vital, for no one could tell how long the *Porpoise* and *Cato* would remain on the reef.

A few moments later, the *Porpoise's* cutter and gig were launched. Both had been so damaged that their occupants had to bail them out with hats and shoes. Flinders jumped overboard and swam to the gig, which was then pushed through the surf to smoother water.

The lights on the *Bridgewater* showed that she was moving away. That forced Flinders to abandon the notion of getting to her. Neither could he return to the *Porpoise,* because she was surrounded by pounding waves and a strong sea current was now surging over the reef. For the moment, his only course was to remain on the smoother waters behind the reef. Suddenly he noticed that the tide was going down. He sighed with relief. The *Porpoise* would now be let down firmly on the reef instead of being lifted over it and sunk in deeper water.

In this helpless situation the night was spent. With a southeast wind blowing fresh and cold, it was a miserable night for the wet and bedraggled crewmen clinging to the broken ships or huddled in little boats.

At the first light of dawn, Flinders clambered up the fallen mast and went on board the *Porpoise,* much to the delight of all aboard, who supposed that the smaller boats had capsized. With a shout of delight they saw the *Bridgewater* far in the distance, sailing toward the reef.

The problem now was to land both crews on the reef, if possible, so that they could be taken aboard the *Bridgewater.* The reef itself was less than a mile wide, and appeared to extend in an east-west direction for as far as they could see. The nearest of several islands was a sandbank barely above high water. If the contents of the ships could be unloaded onto that island, which seemed to have a harbor adjacent, everything could be easily sent aboard the *Bridgewater.*

Flinders ordered the men on the *Porpoise* to carry as much equipment as possible to the reef. There was a constant coming and going as food, supplies, and other equipment were taken to the reef. Aboard the *Cato,* men jumped overboard and swam toward the island. All but three succeeded in reaching it. The three drowned while fighting to get ashore—the only casualties in the entire operation.

Every eye must certainly have glanced from time to time at the distant sails of the *Bridgewater,* for that ship seemed the only means of escaping from this tiny island. But by mid-morning they saw that the sails of the *Bridgewater* were not growing larger at all. They were getting smaller. The ship was sailing away!

The unloading continued, and by night they had gotten the supplies ashore and given clothing to the *Cato's* men. Franklin pitched in with all the rest, one of his principal duties being to herd on shore a number of sheep that had been aboard the *Porpoise.*

Next morning the *Bridgewater* was nowhere in sight.

"Damn me, I'm at a loss to understand that!" Flinders exclaimed in outrage. "How can any captain desert another thus, especially since our wreckage warned him to avoid the reef?"

They had hoisted the Union Jack upside down on a flagstaff as an international signal of distress. If the *Bridgewater's* crew had seen *that* . . .

There was little time to contemplate the matter. The situation on the reef was still serious. Everything on the *Porpoise* had to be gotten ashore, for the ship was stove in beyond repair.

On the other hand, their prospects were not all bad. There were birds and nests, which meant that the sea only rarely, if ever, covered the island. And if worst came to worst, the birds themselves could be eaten.

Discipline had to be maintained, too. Even though he had been a passenger, Flinders was the highest ranking naval officer. With the assent of the other officers, he now took command.

Since some of the 94 survivors were men in His Majesty's service, and some were merchantmen not subject to Admiralty laws, Flinders called a meeting of the entire company to make the situation clear.

"We are wrecked," he began, "but not lost. While God grants an Englishman a breath of freedom he will save himself. To do so, we shall maintain order on this reef as closely as on a ship. I realize that some of you are not in the pay of His Majesty. For the common survival, however, I am assuming command as a magistrate acting within the jurisdiction of the Admiralty. Under that authority I shall punish all deviations from obedience and good order."

John Franklin admired the captain's boldness. It was an example of leadership that he would some day use himself, though he could not have dreamed how often and how steadily he was going to need the ability to lead.

All went well for two days when, as Flinders describes it, "a complaint being made . . . of insolent and discontented expressions used by one of our men to an officer, the articles of war were publicly read and the man punished at the flagstaff. This example served to correct any evil disposition, if such existed: the men worked cordially together, and in all respects we preserved the same discipline . . . as on board His Majesty's ships."

Tents were erected for the stores as well as the men. When the immediate safety of all was assured, the officers turned to a plan of action.

"I propose," said Flinders, "that a six-oared cutter be fitted with supplies and crew to sail to Port Jackson for help."

"How far is it, sir?"

Wreck Reef. An engraving based on an original painting by William Westall. It shows the tents erected by the survivors, and the British ensign flying upside down as a sign of distress. A wrecked vessel, presumably the *Porpoise*, can be seen at the far left

"Our calculations place it at nearly 750 miles."

"Captain, you can't be serious! Across the open sea for such a distance—in a *cutter?*"

"At this season, sir, with contrary winds?"

"Aye," answered Flinders, "it'll be cool work, my lads. While it is being done, the men on the reef must build a new vessel from the timbers of the *Porpoise* and sail to the mainland if the men in the cutter fail."

"And who is to go?" asked another.

"It is a matter for volunteers, my lads."

"Any of us would go, sir—if you would lead."

The others nodded. Flinders said: "So be it. I shall choose among you who will go and who will stay. But understand—the men on this reef are my first concern. If for any reason the men in the cutter do not succeed, then safe conduct of these people ashore must be accomplished in vessels that you are able to construct. God help us all."

Eight days later the cutter, christened *Hope,* was ready to leave.

"Huzzah! Huzzah! Huzzah!" All hands ashore cheered heartily as Flinders and his thirteen men embarked. As they rowed away, a sailor on shore sprang to the flagstaff where the upside-down flag had been flying as a signal of distress, hauled it down and rehoisted it with the union right-side-up. John Franklin could see that this gesture of confidence deeply moved the captain and men on the cutter.

After that, all those on the tiny island silently watched as fair winds filled the little vessel's sails and carried her out to sea.

That night John sat beside a candle in his tent. A soft sea breeze blew over the bank and he could hear the distant murmur of the breakers at the edge of the reef. He took a pen and started a letter to his family. Strange, he thought, to be writing without knowing whether he and his shipmates would be delivered alive from this place. But Flinders would see them through. He was sure of it. He wrote:

"Dear Father, great will be your surprise and sorrow to find by this that the late investigators are cast away in a sandy patch of about 300 yards long and 200 broad, by the wreck of H.M.S. *Porpoise* on our homeward bound passage . . .

"The *Porpoise* being a tough little ship hath, and still does in some measure, resist the power of the waves, and we have been able to get most of her provisions, water, spars, carpenter's tools, and every other necessary on the bank, fortunate spot that it is, on which 94 souls live.

"Captain Flinders and his officers have determined that he and thirteen men should go to Port Jackson in a cutter and fetch a vessel for the remainder; and in the meantime we are to build two boats sufficiently large to contain us if the vessels should not come. Therefore we shall be from this bank in six or eight weeks, and most probably in England by eight or nine. Our loss was more felt as we anticipated the pleasure of seeing our friends and relations after an absence of two years and a half . . ."

Working steadily together, the shipwrecked sailors and merchantmen managed to bring the guns and carriages from the *Porpoise* and place them in a half-moon formation close to the flagstaff. Then, with the laying of a 32-foot keel, construction of the new ship began. Boats went out from time to time as the men hunted turtles, fish, birds, and eggs to supplement their diet.

How often each man must have looked out to sea. Days turned into weeks and the weeks into a month and still nothing could be seen on the horizon but the drifting clouds and multitudes of birds.

They must have begun to fear that the worst had happened to Flinders and his men—a heavy rain . . . high waves that filled the little boat and sank her . . . a violent current that dashed her to pieces against the mainland . . . an attack by the natives . . .

With the coming of October there were murmurings among the men that surely Flinders must have failed, else he would have returned by now. With every passing day, the boat being built on the reef took on greater significance, and before long was fitted with masts and rigging and had, in the words of one of the sailors, the appearance of a rakish schooner. They named her the *Resource*.

As the instruments of navigation had been salvaged from the *Porpoise*, Franklin and others engaged themselves in determining the position of the reef so that no ship in the future would sail near it.

The *Resource*, finally ready to sail, was taken out on October 7 for a short test cruise. During this, one of the seamen observed a strange white object off to the southwest. At first he thought it was a bird, but on closer scrutiny shouted: "Damn my blood, do you see what I see?"

On shore, at almost the same time, the object was sighted by one of the midshipmen who shouted to the nearest officer: "I say, sir, over there—a ship and two schooners!"

Instantly shouts of delight went up from every quarter, and the reef came alive with excitement.

By two o'clock, Captain Flinders had anchored in the lee of the bank and was greeted by an eleven-gun salute from the carronades on shore. He was long and loudly cheered by his grateful shipmates—John Franklin not the least among them—who pressed around to shake his hand

and thank him. Tears of joy rolled down their weather-beaten faces. Flinders said, later: "The pleasure I felt at rejoining the companions of my misfortune, so amply provided with the means of relieving them, cannot be described."

The "means" to which he referred were the three ships he had brought with him: one, the *Rolla,* bound for China; another for those wishing to return to Australia; and the *Cumberland,* in which Flinders himself planned to sail to England.

"The voyage, sir, tell us about the voyage!"

Flinders related how, three days after leaving Wreck Reef in the cutter, they had sighted the Australian mainland and followed southwesterly along the coast. High seas and strong gales forced them to lighten the ship by throwing overboard some food and water. For a while they sailed under favorable winds but soon were beset by lowering weather and were deluged more than once with heavy rain.

They had been forced through shark-infested waters into coves and bights for shelter against the squalls that swept the coast, but at last had reached Port Jackson. Here they received every help from the Governor and the people of Sydney, and soon sailed with the rescue ships.

Flinders arranged the division of the men into ships going in the three directions, and it fell to John Franklin to sail in the *Rolla* for Canton, China.

John dreaded the departure because it meant farewell to Captain Flinders, whom he respected for his knowledge of navigation and leadership, his kindness and fairness. He said goodby with a heavy heart, and could only hope that some day they would sail together again.

Seven

WAR WITH
THE FRENCH

The voyage to China was without incident. In Canton, John joined a merchant fleet and was soon at sea again, sailing toward England with Commodore Nathaniel Dance. And sailing toward danger, too, for once more war had erupted.

The peace established by the Treaty of Amiens, which Flinders and his men and the French had celebrated at Port Jackson, had not lasted long. Napoleon had merely used the temporary peace to get his country running smoothly again, and to stock up his arsenals with weapons for more wars.

He had conquered Europe already, and stood on the verge of making France the most powerful nation in the world. All Napoleon had to do, it seemed, was crush England, get rid of that infernal British Navy, and then take over the rich trade routes to the East and West Indies.

That "infernal" British Navy had given Napoleon no end of trouble. His armies on land won battle after battle, but at sea his fleet was forever getting pummeled by the English—and mostly by Lord Nelson. Worse yet, Nelson kept Napoleon's fleet besieged, blockaded, trapped in port. The Frenchmen couldn't sail, they couldn't maneuver, they couldn't practice, they couldn't fight. All they could do was fret and fume.

And without a navy, how would Napoleon's 150,000-man invasion army move across the English Channel? Even now the army was poised on the cliffs above Boulogne, ready to move. All Napoleon needed was to wrest his fleet away from Nelson, and England would be his!

Not all of France's Navy was besieged, however, for in the Strait of Malacca that 15th of February, 1804, Admiral Linois closed in upon a "helpless" British merchant fleet.

No one knew better than Commodore Dance how dangerous it was—lightly armed as were most merchant fleets those days—to sail through waters known to be occupied by the enemy. Further, he must have known that a powerful French squadron under Admiral Linois would almost certainly leave Batavia to intercept British ships attempting to force a passage through the narrow strait.

Considering the odds against the English, the French must have awaited the battle gleefully. Admiral Linois, as he sighted the ships on the horizon, must have been amused that the clever English would sail so weak a squadron squarely into his arms.

As he stood on the deck of Commodore Dance's flagship, John Franklin had a chilling thought. If Admiral Linois *did* win, he would take these merchant prizes back to Napoleon as a gift. With the money they would bring, Napoleon could build a dozen or more landing craft to ferry his invasion army across the English Channel. John shuddered at the thought of Lincolnshire being overrun, or of Spilsby being taken by the French.

Napoleon's invaders seemed real enough, but at the moment those approaching battleships were more so. The battle was going to be uneven. John knew it. Commodore Dance had fifteen ships, but none was fully geared for battle. The French had five—all warships—armed to the gunwales. Why then, John wondered, was Dance sailing boldly toward the French, especially this late in the afternoon? Was it daring or madness? Or was it both?

John had little time for speculation. His job as signal midshipman was to hoist the signal flags which, when viewed by other ships under the commodore's command, would tell the captains of those ships exactly what to do.

The orders began to come rapidly. Just as rapidly John selected and attached the flags, and ran them up into the breeze. Very soon, the merchant fleet had formed in line of battle. The French must have wondered what was going on. Merchant ships in line of battle? Absurd! They usually clapped on sail and fled at the sight of enemy warships. Why not now?

Seeing the British braced for battle and the sun about to set, the French hauled to the wind and stood off at a distance. Oho! thought John. They're puzzled by these battle movements of the British ships. They suspect a trick.

Night fell, and the French must have expected the British merchantmen to sneak away. But next morning they were there, and still in order of battle!

John had no doubt about it now. Commodore Dance was bluffing, trying to mystify the French by simple pluck and daring. He wanted them to think that he was far more powerful than he was. Already he had them guessing, and he hoped they'd guess that some of his merchant ships were men-of-war disguised.

So far, it had worked. At dawn, Admiral Linois should have attacked. He didn't. He hesitated. In a gesture of contempt, Dance ordered Franklin to raise the signal for continuation of previous course under easy sail. Franklin

Sir Nathaniel Dance, in uniform of the East India Company

laughed aloud as he got the flags together. It was as if Dance were ignoring Linois entirely. What effrontery!

As the British ships resumed their course, Linois moved to cut off part of them. That was what Dance had been waiting for. Immediately he ordered hoisted the flag that Franklin had eagerly hoped to send up: "Tack in succession, bear down in line ahead, and engage the enemy."

Cheers rang out on the British ships. Engage the enemy! It seemed as ludicrous an engagement as had ever been fought on the high seas. It didn't seem possible that the British would not be annihilated.

Firing began, and soon the action became general: lobbing cannonballs, acrid smoke, smashing wood, and flying splinters. The contest continued sharply for nearly an hour, after which the French apparently decided that they had sailed into more than they could handle. Accordingly they withdrew and sailed away.

Seeing this, Dance ordered John to hoist the flag that signaled every British ship to pour on sail and join in pursuit. For two hours the chase continued; then Dance formed the squadron to sail for England. The French, undoubtedly much chagrined at being routed by simple merchantmen, but daring not to risk more action, disappeared and did not molest the British again.

On August 6, 1804, John Franklin arrived in England. It had been three years since he had seen those familiar sea cliffs and the warm and friendly countryside beyond. In three years he had almost forgotten the smell of the fens and wolds of Lincolnshire, though he and his shipmates had often talked about them. Now as he rode in the post chaise up the dusty path to Spilsby, he was more excited than when he had returned as a hero of Copenhagen. Now he was a hero of Australia, of a shipwreck, and of a battle in the Strait of Malacca.

How excitedly little Henrietta must have sat at his knee and listened to his stories. For that matter, the entire family must have been enthralled by his adventures.

But there was news for John, too—first about the ship *Bridgewater,* which had deserted them on Wreck Reef. When the ship arrived in port, her captain tried to convince authorities that he had found it impossible to get to the reef and that in any case it would have been too late to render assistance to the men of the *Porpoise* and *Cato.*

This wasn't true, John thought, angrily, and the captain knew it. But no matter. Shortly afterward the *Bridgewater* left Bombay for London and was never seen again.

John then asked about Captain Flinders, and learned to his dismay that Flinders' ship had been taken by the French at the Isle of Mauritius, off the eastern coast of Africa, and Flinders made a prisoner.

It seemed impossible! Flinders was an explorer. He had a passport from the French. They could not detain him . . .

But they had. John's anger must have risen to new levels. Was there no one to stop this madman, Napoleon?

The British expected that Napoleon, having conquered so much of Europe, would attempt to invade England itself, and there was great fear throughout the land. Yet Franklin knew, and every Englishman knew, that the only means of stopping that invasion—and even of stopping Napoleon himself—was a half-blind British Admiral named Horatio Nelson.

Nelson! The very sound of his name must have thrilled Midshipman Franklin. Nelson was so much a hero that many a red-blooded British lad wanted to sail and to fight under him.

Franklin knew what it was like, for he remembered Nelson's daring at Copenhagen. At the moment, Nelson was in command of the Mediterranean. For some time he had been off Toulon, where the French fleet, under Admiral Villeneuve, lay at anchor. In a sense, he was blockading the port, but the fact was that he *wanted* Villeneuve to sail. That was Nelson's way. If only he could get those French ships to come out and fight!

Again, the thought of it captured John's imagination. He had served with Flinders and learned to navigate and to explore. He wanted more of that. And, like any sailor, he also longed for fighting action.

Well, he was soon to report for duty on the warship *Bellerophon*. Rumor had it that she was going south to join Nelson. Perhaps then they would get a sea battle out of Napoleon. If the combined fleets of France and Spain would only sail—Nelson would give them a drubbing the like of which they had never got before. What a fight it would be!

And how John Franklin would like to be there . . .

Eight

TRAFALGAR

"Clear the ship for action!"

The boatswain's shout was repeated at all hatchways to the lower decks of the *Bellerophon*. The ship came alive.

"Today's the day!"

"Stow hammocks!"

"Sling the lower yards!"

John Franklin sprang out of bed, knelt briefly for a prayer, hurried into his clothes, and clambered up on the quarterdeck.

There they were on the horizon—the fleets of France and Spain, a forest of masts to the leeward. He counted them—thirty-three ships of the line, all formidable battleships, their gun ports open and ready. Beyond them, hazy on the horizon, lay the cliffs of Cape Trafalgar . . . the coast of Spain.

He had seen a lot of the Spanish coast these past few months, and the French as well. The previous winter, after he had been assigned to her, the warship *Bellerophon* had blockaded the French in the harbor of Brest. When summer came his squadron sailed for Cadiz and took up there the task of confining other units of the fleets of France and Spain.

Cadiz was a picturesque seaport lying sixty miles northwest of Gibraltar. In between lay Cape Trafalgar, an Atlantic headland that shimmered in the distance on this bright but hazy October day in 1805.

Here at last the enemies faced each other at sea. No longer did the French and Spanish fleet hide away in Cadiz. There it lay on the horizon, ready to fight. This was the moment Nelson and every sailor with him had been hoping, praying, and waiting for.

"Avast, mates! Yonder lies the enemy. Jump to the deck!"

"Rouse out and look alive!"

John raced below with all the others, rolled and tied his bedding, and with it ran again topside.

They had good reason for stowing the bedding on the upper decks. Each side of the quarterdeck and poop was furnished with a double network of ropes, supported by iron cranes atop the gunwale. The bed rolls snugly stored there formed a padded barrier against small shot from enemy guns. Similarly, padded bulwarks were thrown up against the tops, the waist, and the forecastle.

Commands came from all decks. Men ran in every direction, attending to their specific duties. John, as signal midshipman, took his station on the poop, and from there watched the vessel galvanize into action. Everything was working as smoothly as the clock-work in the chronometers, which was exactly as Captain Cooke would have it. John had liked Cooke from the first day he had come aboard and taken command of the *Bellerophon*. "Very gentlemanly and active," he had written to his mother of the captain. "I like his appearance much."

He also liked the ship. The *Bellerophon,* a 74-gun battleship, had led Admiral Howe's fleet to victory on the "glorious first of June," in 1794, during a battle with the French in the English Channel. Later she had fought the

French in the Battle of the Nile. Now, as she sailed once more against the enemy, the six hundred men aboard her were taking their stations as the ship prepared for battle.

John put his telescope to his eye. Nelson's flagship, *Victory,* sails full, flags flying, led the opposite line of vessels. John was to watch that ship for orders, and also to watch for signal flags from the leader of his own line, Admiral Collingwood in the *Royal Sovereign.*

Franklin had beside him the secret signal code book, from which he could tell what flags to hoist as well as the meaning of signals hoisted on other ships.

Into his pocket he had thrust another book, a small brown one that he'd been carefully reading for months. It was titled *Naval Tactics.* In it were diagrams in color of various ship and squadron movements, things every sea officer needed to know. There were definitions of naval terms, orders of sailing, combat maneuvers, and orders of battle.

As he stood beside the signal rope he remembered one of the passages in the book: "The art of war at sea," it read, "is limited by the possibilities of navigation; and is therefore much less capable of that variety of stratagem which belongs to the hostility of armies."

How true, he thought. Armies could move so easily overland. They could hide when they needed to. Here at sea each ship could be seen for miles, and it lay at the mercy of wind and weather and waves.

"But although the naval warrior," the book continued, "cannot place his fleet in ambush, nor at all times press the foe in their weakest part, let it not be supposed that contrivance and surprise are excluded from this mode of battle. No: on the contrary, they are often the protection of inferior force, and frequently end the contest of equal powers.

"So—much greater must be the talents and more acute the ingenuity of him who can devise and execute an unexpected manoeuvre. To do this, belongs to genius: it cannot be learned from books, for the moment of invention is the moment of execution."

John repeated that phrase. It was the mark of a good sea captain. It was certainly Nelson's trademark . . . boldness . . . surprise . . . using every moment to its fullest advantage.

"Drummer!" the lieutenant shouted. "Beat *To Quarters.*"

They had now begun to bear down upon the enemy ships. The staccato drumbeat burst across the ship and below to the gun decks. Activity that had seemed so frantic earlier now took on an orderly appearance.

Seamen flung sand across the deck to give better grip to running feet—for the decks would soon be slippery with blood. The decks were also watered down to reduce the hazard of fire. The cook doused fires in the galley; all hands would henceforth have cold meals.

Men stripped to the waist, anticipating the heat of battle, and wrapped cloth around their heads to keep out some of the noise of exploding guns. Everything loose that might be hurled into the air they lashed to the deck or stored in the hold. They secured sail yards. They collected shot plugs for filling holes that would soon be blasted in the sides of the vessel. They readied tools for repair of masts and sails and rigging when these were shot away.

No longer did John wear his blue tail-coat that was lined with silk. No longer had he his waistcoat and breeches of white nankeen, or the three-cornered hat with gold loop and cockade. Gone was the black silk handkerchief from his neck and the shirt of frilled linen. Others

might fight in their uniforms; he preferred old clothes.
He had, in fact, worn his uniform rarely. Life on a
seagoing man-of-war was seldom as formal as on shore.
Being an experienced midshipman, he did not have to
sling his hammock in the gun room as the beginners did,
or attend the classes in navigation. His quarters were in
the midshipmen's berth on the orlop deck, where he ate
with the older midshipmen and with the lieutenants.

It was a good life. While they were on sea or blockade
duty, he had had instruction in advanced navigation. He
had taken readings of the sun at noon and plotted the
positions of the ships, as he had done for Flinders. Often
and swiftly he climbed to the topmasts to supervise the
furling of the mizzen royal and other sails. Or, that is to
say, he went as swiftly as his portly frame could carry
him; his friends were all surprised that one as heavy as he
could move so easily.

"Steady as she goes," the lieutenant said quietly. The
two fleets were drawing closer.

At last came the beat of the drum and the shout of the
lieutenant. "To arms! To arms!"

The order was repeated by deck lieutenants below.
Immediately the cannon were loaded, and their muzzles
run out through the gun ports. The *Bellerophon* bristled
like a deadly mace. Its guns protruded on both sides in
rows of menacing muzzles, waiting for the enemy ships to
come within range.

By now the French and Spanish fleets were near
enough for John to see men moving on their decks. He
could also see that through their gun ports the muzzles of
their cannon were trained on the British warships.

It seemed to him that a sea of canvas lay all around—
from horizon to horizon. Never had he seen so many ships

—not in Copenhagen, or Port Jackson, or the Strait of Malacca. There were 33 enemy warships, lying on the beam, spread out directly athwart the path of the 27 British vessels. (The British had other ships—four frigates, a schooner, and a cutter—but these were not counted as vessels engaged in the actual fighting.) The British had not lined up as precisely as they should—John saw that. But it would have to do. The two fleets were now locked into position and the space between them was growing smaller. They had reached the point of no return.

The enemy ships seemed almost to be waiting proudly as the two lines of British sails bore down upon them. They were formidable enough. One of them, the Spanish *Santissima Trinidad,* had 130 guns and a crew of 1,048— the largest warship in the world.

For the sailors aboard the *Bellerophon* it was a tense moment as they neared the point of contact. Some sharpened their cutlasses. Some polished their muskets. Some chalked on the guns: *"Bellerophon—Death or Glory."* Below, John could hear someone dancing a hornpipe.

"Steady," came the quiet orders of the lieutenant. "Starboard a little. As she goes . . ."

Light winds carried them slowly but inexorably forward. A dinner of cold meat was passed around at 11:00. Shortly before noon the order came to "make ready."

A series of metallic clicks sounded along the gun decks as flintlocks were cocked. Gun captains crouched and held taut the trigger-lines that connected to the flintlocks. Sweat trickled down the naked backs of the crewmen as they waited.

At this moment, the ship's band began to play. Fiddles and fifes and drums sent their rousing notes into the air, and from the other ships could also be heard the playing of bands. Sailors shouted and laughed across the water.

Suddenly John snapped to attention. Signal flags were being run up the *Victory's* mast. It was Nelson's last order before the battle.

"England . . . expects . . . that every man . . . will do his duty."

Wasn't that like Nelson? John beamed. Those were words to fight by. "The signal, sir," he said to the lieutenant. "England expects that every man will do his duty."

Next up the *Victory's* mast went flags number one and six. John knew that signal well. The whole fleet had been awaiting it.

"Engage the enemy!"

Captain Cooke himself immediately went below to read to his men the message from Nelson. As he did so, shouts and cheers erupted from the gun crews. In a few moments, the captain returned to the poop.

John looked overhead, and then to the other ships. From the *Bellerophon* and from the main-topmast of every ship in the fleet, the Union Jack waved lazily in the easy breeze. The ships were close enough—why didn't they fire?

Then, from the corner of his eye, he beheld a burst of orange fire fly out from one of the enemy vessels nearest the *Victory*. The battle had begun!

Nelson held his response until the *Victory* was nearly upon the French ships. Then he fired. From left and right the guns of the *Victory* thundered with a mighty roar, sending broadsides toward the enemy ships. Shot fell like rain and smashed into the French, and the *Victory* in turn was raked by a devastating volley.

The other British ships sailed into range and started

shooting. John watched the firing through his telescope, saw rigging ripped into shreds and sails cut to tatters. He saw men mowed down until they fell in heaps upon the decks. In the first few minutes, the leading ships took on the appearance of slaughter houses.

The ships in his own line began to fire, and then it was the *Bellerophon's* turn. At 12:20 she entered the battle.

Midshipmen ran below with orders for the lieutenants of the gun decks, who leaped back from the muzzles and shouted: "Fire!"

"Fire!" Down every deck the same command was echoed. Trigger lines jerked. Carronades leaped with a roar and the gun trucks recoiled with a rumble and clatter. Fire exploded from the ports and yellow-tinged clouds blew out over the water. Gunsmoke whipped backward, in from the ports, creating a stifling pall that seared the lungs and nearly choked the gunners. It also blotted out the light, after which the decks became chaotic. In the darkness, every gun crew feverishly worked to sponge out its gun and reload, to ram the cartridge home, jam in the shot, the wad, and more shot, cock the locks, and jump back.

"Fire!"

First the starboard side let go, and then the larboard. The *Bellerophon* had pierced the enemy line and now there were hostile ships on every side.

From his vantage point, John saw that the *Bellerophon* was caught in a forest of canvas, with four enemy ships pouring death into her. Whizzing shot tore away sails, ripping them from the booms, pocking them with holes. It-tore up deck planking, cut hammocks to ribbons, hurled guns off their carriages. Splinters flew through the air like shot, cutting and gouging human flesh. Men fell everywhere.

Great clouds of flying lead smashed into the *Bellerophon*. Out of the smoke and haze John saw a French ship so close that he could read her name: the *Aigle*. With a crash, the *Bellerophon* collided with her and, after that, bedlam reigned as the two ships "engaged with the utmost fury."

French sharpshooters swept the decks of the *Bellerophon* with a hail of musket fire. Grenade throwers hid behind the *Aigle's* masts and hurled their weapons.

Men shouted until they were hoarse. Smoke swirled into their eyes. On the *Bellerophon* powder men scrambled frantically from magazines to guns. A group of marines, crouched behind the bulwarks on the poop, laid a withering fire across the *Aigle's* decks, forcing her soldiers to leap for cover and to crouch behind the rail.

Below, the *Bellerophon's* carronades, firing point blank, blasted great holes into the French ship.

As John stood on the quarterdeck, scores of men around him were cut down by musket shot, grenade fragments, and splinters. Captain Cooke stood with smoking pistols, firing into the men on the *Aigle's* quarterdeck. All at once two musket balls struck him and in a minute he lay dead where he had crumpled to the deck.

"It's the captain!" a quartermaster shouted. "Captain Cooke's been bowl'd out!"

Midshipmen, running here and there, fell wounded or dead from the vicious fragments. Suddenly, a boom of cannon and a deafening crash shook the ship. John staggered. A piercing pain filled his head. Dull humming seemed all at once to drown out every other noise in his ears. For a while it seemed as if the sounds of battle were far away. But they soon came back. His hearing returned a little, but the ache and humming continued.

"*A l'abordage*!" yelled the French officers, urging their men on to the *Bellerophon*.

"Board her!" shouted the British officers. "Attack!"

Hand to hand fighting now became general. Below decks, gun crews of both ships fought from porthole to porthole, swinging their cutlasses and firing their muskets. Several Frenchmen, swords waving, swung onto the *Bellerophon* and clambered along the bowsprit, but a quick-acting British seaman loosened the yard on which they were approaching and dumped them into the sea.

John saw Frenchmen leap across the gap between the ships, clinging to whatever they could—only to have their hands and fingers whacked by British marines. One by one the enemy soldiers fell into the ocean.

Other ships closed in, hitting the *Bellerophon* from all sides. John heard a cracking and splintering, and looked up to see the mainmast toppling. Down it came with a terrific crash, carrying a mass of shredded sails and tangled rigging with it. No sooner had this canvas fallen in front of the gun ports than the flash of the cannons set it ablaze.

Fire! It was the greatest dread of sailors at sea. Quickly Lieutenant Cumby, now in command, ordered the sail cut free. Men leaped forward with axes and cutlasses and chopped away the burning sail, which fell with a hiss into the sea.

By now the *Bellerophon's* decks were a shambles, an "unmanageable wreck" as the lieutenant told the crews below. But gunfire on both ships had slowed. On the *Bellerophon* nearly thirty men had died already; another hundred and twenty lay wounded.

Aside from keeping his eyes trained far away for signal flags, John watched for sharpshooters among the masts of the *Aigle*.

"Ahoy, Simmonds," he shouted, beckoning to another midshipman.

"What is it, old man?" asked the other, coming up.

"We must pick off those sharpshooters," John said. "Look, over there in the foretop of the *Aigle*. That one! See how he wears a cocked hat. I've seen him already shoot several of our— Watch out!"

A musket shot rang out and Simmonds spun away, falling to the deck.

John crawled to him, but it was too late. The midshipman was dead.

"Sir!" came a voice above the din. "Would you help?"

Franklin turned and saw a marine sergeant crouching over an injured seaman.

"He's still alive, sir," said the sergeant.

Franklin grasped the injured man by the shoulders. "Let's take him below." As they picked him up and started off, another musket sounded from the foretop of the *Aigle,* and a ball pierced the injured seaman's heart— killing him as Franklin and the sergeant carried him to safety.

"He'll have you next," Franklin exclaimed as they laid the seaman beside a hatchway.

"Indeed he will not!" The sergeant scowled bitterly. "Take cover! I'm going back to get my musket. I'll not stop firing till I blow that rascal off his cocky perch."

The sergeant disappeared. Franklin made his way back to the quarterdeck, keeping an eye on the sharpshooter. Suddenly the Frenchman raised the musket and aimed straight at him. Almost as the weapon fired, Franklin leaped behind a mast, the musket ball plowing into the deck a scant few feet behind him.

"Meantime," as he later described the scene in a letter to his family, "so few guns were being discharged that I could hear the sergeant firing away with his musket from below. Looking out from behind the mast I saw the rifle-man, whose features I vow I shall never forget so long as I live, fall headforemost into the sea."

In a moment the sergeant came up.

"How many times did you fire?" Franklin asked.

The sergeant's smudged face twisted into a grim smile. "I killed him at the seventh shot," he said.

The *Aigle* had had enough. As she drifted away, the *Bellerophon* poured more broadsides into her until she vanished in the smoke and haze. By 4:30 the battle was over. Surveying the scene, Franklin saw a fearful sight of waste and destruction. Debris floated on the water for as far as he could see: ropes, sails, masts, planking . . . In the distance lay vessels disabled, afire, or—in the case of the French and Spanish—fleeing. One French ship blew up. Small boats bore British captains to take possession of enemy ships that had struck their colors in surrender.

Recognizing the signs, Franklin could tell beyond all trace of doubt that England had won. More than that, she had won the greatest battle in which she had ever engaged, or in fact, the greatest sea action fought anywhere. What a sight it was!

The fleets of France and Spain lay ruined. The British had destroyed or captured eighteen vessels—the others were escaping to Cadiz—while not a single British ship had been sunk, or had even surrendered. The world would later learn that 4,408 Frenchmen and Spaniards had died that day off Cape Trafalgar. The British lost 449 men. Thousands more had been wounded. Of those who stood near Franklin on the poop of the *Bellerophon,* all except four or five were either killed or wounded.

Signals were being hoisted. He shook his head. That dull humming and pain still throbbed in his ears. Flags on the *Victory* were being raised on makeshift staffs.

As he read the signals, John turned pale. He froze at what he saw. He couldn't believe it. Yet there went the flags, one by one, with their terrible message.

"Lord Nelson is dead."

Scene on the flagship *Victory* at the moment of Nelson's fall during the battle of Trafalgar (from an oil painting by D. Dighton)

Nine

NEW ORLEANS

The news stunned the fleet. The Admiral, shot by an enemy sharpshooter, had died at 4:30, almost immediately after learning of the great victory.

Franklin himself felt wounded by the news, as if struck by a volley of shot from enemy cannon. But what could be done? Nelson was gone. An age of sailing and fighting would go with him. Nothing remained but to carry on, to take home the captured ships, to repair the wounds . . .

With heavy hearts, the fighting men of Nelson's fleet set sadly to work. Seamen repaired the masts and yards and patched the sails, knotted and spliced the rigging, plugged the hull holes, and repaired and refitted the cannon.

On the day after the battle a violent storm blew the tattered remnants of the fleet toward land and wrecked a few of the captured ships. When fleeing enemy vessels rammed into shore, men drowned by the hundreds. Then, as the gale abated, the battered British fleet made its way to Gibraltar and anchored.

The Battle of Trafalgar was over, and it *was* the last great sea battle in the age of sail. So completely had Nelson destroyed the enemy fleets that Napoleon never again came close to ruling the world.

In the years that followed, therefore, the Royal Navy

had little more than patrol duty to offer its sailors. Franklin, now in his twenties, was assigned to the warship *Bedford,* which spent more than two years off the coast of South America. Another voyage took him to the islands of Madeira, and still another to the coast of Holland.

During this time the young midshipman did so well in his studies of the sea and of navigation that he was promoted to master's mate and then to lieutenant. Often he recalled the days with Captain Flinders in Australia. How he would like to explore like that again! He had not forgotten, either, that Flinders was still a prisoner of war on the isle of Mauritius.

Would the war ever end? Napoleon, even with his fleets destroyed, still strove to conquer Europe. But now new trouble rose to plague him: Spain had begun to revolt. Without Spain, Napoleon's empire might start crumbling to pieces.

In 1807, John's eldest brother died in Spilsby, and three years later his mother died. In 1810, also, word came that Captain Flinders had been freed and had arrived in England. But the captain and his ex-midshipman never met again.

As the years went by, with no sea battles to fight, Lieutenant Franklin asked himself: "What's the use of being in the Navy?" He studied and worked as hard as ever, but he began to grow impatient.

By 1813, Napoleon's empire was collapsing, following the loss of Germany and a disastrous venture into Russia. It began to look as if peace were coming and there were to be no wars at all.

But those whose minds ran that way were forgetting the young and impetuous country on the other side of the Atlantic Ocean—the United States. The Americans had

been trying to stay neutral in the war between Britain and
France, but the way Britain treated their ships and seamen made them boiling mad. Moreover, settlers in the
western part of the United States (at that time the "West"
ended at the Mississippi River) became angry because
they thought the British were stirring up trouble with the
Indians and causing them hard times. They wanted war.

In 1812 they got it.

Like any young sailor yearning for action, Franklin
must have been delighted. "Now that the Americans have
declared war on us," he thought, "we shall have some
fighting. We shall show those ragged upstarts a thing or
two!"

The *Bedford* was fitted out for a voyage to the West
Indies, and before long sailed across the Gulf of Mexico
toward New Orleans. The British had tried to invade the
United States before. They had entered Canada, but were
defeated on Lake Champlain, in New York. They had
attacked Washington, D.C., and had even set the White
House and Capitol afire, but were stopped by the defenses
at Fort McHenry, near Baltimore.

Now they had another chance. All they had to do was
invade New Orleans and capture control of the Mississippi River. How could they fail? Their troops were
trained and experienced. The Americans were largely un-
trained, and there were not many of them. Besides, Napoleon's empire had collapsed and now that the British
didn't have to fight France any more they could turn their
full attention to America.

Thus it was that Lieutenant Franklin found himself
approaching the Battle of New Orleans. No doubt he
shared the general British feeling that this would be an
easy victory.

The way to New Orleans lay across Lake Borgne, but since the lake was too shallow for the ships to proceed very far into it, the men were loaded into barges. The British hoped that this action would take the Americans by surprise. But the Americans were not so easily surprised.

On December 13, 1814, with a thousand officers and men on fifty barges—one of which was probably commanded by Franklin—the British moved across the lake. Suddenly, five well-armed American cutters appeared.

Franklin could see instantly that the British were at a

Battle of Lake Borgne showing some of the 50 British barges attacking the high-masted American ships

disadvantage. Nevertheless, in the face of sustained and heavy fire, they rowed their barges closer. Men on both sides staggered under the impact of deadly musket fire and fell into the water. Powder smoke blew across the lake.

The British propelled their barges steadily until the fleets collided. Guns and swords held high, the British sprang up onto the American vessels and plunged into battle, sabering their way to the right and left, cutting, slashing, and firing.

Hope quickly disappeared for the Americans, whose flags were soon hauled down and replaced by the British ensign. Franklin himself was wounded in the shoulder during this battle. But they had won! They had captured the American defenses on Lake Borgne. New Orleans now lay helpless.

The British began their final attack at dawn on January 8, 1815. Other skirmishes and battles following Lake Borgne had cleared the way and brought 5,400 crack British troops to face 4,000 American frontiersmen, Indians, Negroes, sailors, pirates, and a few regular soldiers.

The battle took place on the eastern shore of the Mississippi River, a short way downstream from New Orleans. General Andrew Jackson and his American forces waited behind ramparts as the red-coated British, under a young general named Pakenham, advanced in the early morning light.

Franklin and a group of other sailors, commanded by Colonel Thornton, marched north along the opposite, or western, bank of the Mississippi. This party consisted of about 400 men. They faced three times as many Americans. Moreover, the Americans had heavier arms—especially artillery—with which to defend themselves.

General Sir Edward Michael Pakenham, after a lithograph of an original painting in England

"Charge!"

At the colonel's signal, Franklin and the other sailors rushed ahead. Up the embankment they charged, directly into furious musket and artillery fire. Shouting and firing as they ran, they swept up and over the ramparts and in among the confused and retreating Americans.

Franklin escaped without a scratch, but in the hail of musket balls, his commander was badly wounded.

It didn't take long to rout the Americans and capture their artillery. Without hesitation, the British prepared to turn these guns across the Mississippi. That was their mission: to fire upon Jackson's forces from this side of the river and thus support their comrades in the major battle.

Across the river, however, the British were meeting disaster. General Pakenham had flung his troops directly against the American rampart, and that was his mistake. Whatever these Kentucky and Tennessee frontiersmen lacked in military training they made up for in deadly aim. So accurate was their fire that scores of British soldiers were killed.

Again and again the British generals tried to rally their troops and lead them into fresh attack. Again and again American artillery and musket fire tore vicious holes in the neatly parading British ranks. One by one, the British officers were shot. General Pakenham, riding fearlessly to the front of his troops and urging them on, was struck by flying lead and died before his men could carry him to the rear of the line. His death turned confusion into terror, and terror into panic.

Franklin and his fellow Britons west of the river saw what was happening, and knew the battle was lost. Franklin turned his head and closed his eyes in anger. New Orleans had been within their grasp. Victory had been assured. Now the British forces across the river were falling back in disarray, fleeing and returning to their ships.

Saddened, sick with humiliation, Franklin and his comrades turned and went back to join their bedraggled comrades aboard the *Bedford*. After that, the British fleet raised anchor, loosed canvas, and sailed for home.

The Battle of New Orleans was to be the last great battle ever fought between the United States and England. For Lieutenant Franklin and his countrymen it was perhaps the worst defeat of all. The British had outnumbered the Americans. Their troops had been far superior in training. They had had more experience in warfare. Yet when the casualties were counted, the British had lost two thousand men and the Americans thirteen.

Ten

NORTH TO THE ARCTIC

When Lieutenant Franklin arrived in England in the spring of 1815 he learned that his old captain, Matthew Flinders, had died. Flinders had written two large volumes describing the voyage of the *Investigator* to and around Australia. These volumes, with engravings by William Westall, as well as maps and charts, were titled *Voyage to Terra Australis*. On the day they were published, in 1814, Flinders had died.

Reading the books, Franklin relived every experience of that voyage, as he had done many times before. There was a special appendix on the errors of the compass arising from attractions within the ship.

John remembered how often they had tried to reduce those variations. Flinders had persisted. On arriving in England he got permission from the Admiralty to conduct experiments on other ships. He tried to find some single way to correct all the observations that had been made on the *Investigator*. This led to a study of records from other voyages and the matching of charts of various explorers. While he never quite got to the solution of the problem, he did suggest the fixing of upright iron bars in the stern to counteract attraction of iron elsewhere within a vessel. Not until after his death was an upright bar installed adjacent to the compass. That bar, still in use on ships today, was named the *Flinders Bar*—in honor of the persistent and curious navigator who searched for the answer to compass variations and all but found it.

The year following Flinders' death, the battle of Waterloo was fought in Belgium. That was the end of Napoleon's empire. Less than a year after that, Napoleon surrendered to the English aboard Franklin's old ship, the *Bellerophon,* which had been at Trafalgar.

At the same time, a new chain of circumstances was being forged that would affect the rest of Franklin's life, would make him famous, and would bring him action and excitement such as he had never known. He had never gotten over his great desire to go exploring again. Now he learned that an expedition was about to leave for the North Pole.

Ever since the Greek navigator Pytheas sailed into the North about 320 B.C.—the first sailor known to have traveled from the civilized world to the Arctic Circle—men have been drawn by the fascination of the polar regions. For many centuries little was known of these regions. About the year 870 A.D. the Vikings, courageous seamen of Norway, discovered Iceland and, a hundred years after, were swept past Iceland by storms, thus discovering Greenland. Later, they found Canada. They also sailed to the east, around the Kola Peninsula, into the White Sea, and along the frigid northern coast of Russia.

Centuries later other explorers sailed northward, returned and told their stories, and it began to seem that a northern route to China could be found. China—or Cathay, as it had been known for many years—was a magic name. It was a land of dreams, a land of mystery, a land of enormous riches, of silks and spices and wonderful goods that were not to be had in all of Europe.

But to get to Cathay ships had to sail all the way down to the southern tip of Africa and then across the Indian Ocean. That was too far and, besides, those routes were Spanish and Portuguese trading routes.

What if some other passage to China could be found, some way around the north and west, perhaps beyond Greenland? North and west of England. That was it—a *northwest passage* to Cathay! There might also be a northeast passage, through Arctic seas, across the top of Russia, and down to China. Either way would be far better than having to sail around Africa.

So men began to hunt for a northwest and a northeast passage over the top of the world to Cathay. As early as 1508 or 1509 Sebastian Cabot searched the coasts of Labrador for a strait that might lead to Cathay. He failed. In 1553, Sir Hugh Willoughby was wrecked on the Kola Peninsula where he and his men—one by one—died in the cruel northern winter.

It was not an easy land. Strong icy winds blew out of the east. Storms swept down from the north. Angry seas, studded with icebergs, smashed the frail ships. Yet men set out again and again: Martin Frobisher, John Davis, William Barents, Henry Hudson, and William Baffin—to name a few. Some found an opening, so they thought, to the Northwest Passage (or the Northeast Passage). But no one had, as yet, gone through.

In howling winds and churning seas, they kept on trying. None doubted that the Northwest Passage was there, free of ice, its waters deep and navigable.

Except . . . where was it?

Others than merchants wanted to know. By the eighteenth century, nearly everyone wanted to know. Men of science predicted that new discoveries would be made in the Arctic, and the voyages of Vitus Bering (1741) and James Cook (1778) proved they were right.

The pressure grew so great that in 1745 the British Parliament offered a reward of £20,000 for discovery of the Northwest Passage. The greatest fear now was that some nation other than England would make the final, successful search.

No one was sure what the newly developing country of Russia would do. In 1817, Secretary of the Admiralty John Barrow wrote: "The Russians have for some time been strongly impressed with the idea of an open passage round America . . . It would be somewhat mortifying if a naval power but of yesterday should complete a discovery in the nineteenth century, which was so happily commenced by Englishmen in the sixteenth."

Barrow was convinced, with the wars at an end, that the time had come to solve the mysteries of the Arctic. And what better way than to use the Navy—whose sailors currently had no one to fight?

William Scoresby, the explorer, reported that thousands of square miles of ice had recently melted in the northern seas. Such favorable conditions must be taken advantage of! With this news, Barrow went to the First Lord of the Admiralty, and asked to engage two voyages "for the advancement of geography, navigation, and commerce." The Admiralty approved.

One voyage, led by Commander John Ross and Lieutenant Edward Parry, was to seek an entrance to the Northwest Passage. The other was to sail past Spitsbergen and as near the North Pole as it could, then go through

Bering Strait and south into the Pacific Ocean. Command of this expedition was assigned to Captain David Buchan, a veteran Labrador explorer.

Captain Buchan had two ships, both built for whaling and strengthened for Arctic duty. He made the *Dorothea* his flagship. To command the smaller *Trent,* a 250-ton brig, the Admiralty selected a young lieutenant who had just turned thirty-one, who knew his way around the world, and who had studied as hard as he could to master mathematics and the art of sailing—John Franklin.

"Our orders are clear, Lieutenant," said Captain Buchan, spreading out maps in his cabin. "We must force our way through the ice between Spitsbergen and Greenland. Utmost effort must be made to get to the North Pole —which no one has ever reached."

He traced a route across the wide white space marked *Terra Incognita,* unknown land. "When we reach the Pole we are to remain a few days, if the weather be suitable, to take scientific observations, then continue on through Bering Strait. If we arrive in Kamchatka, we shall call upon the Russian Governor and provide him with our full reports to be transported overland to England. Following that, we sail to the Sandwich Islands, or some other suitable place to refresh our crew, and return the way we went—through the Northwest Passage."

By April, 1818, the *Dorothea* and *Trent* were nearly ready to leave. All England, it seemed to Franklin, was excited by the voyage.

"I find it quite impossible to believe," he said to his first lieutenant, Frederick Beechey, a short, dark-eyed young man with golden hair, "the amazing interest our little squadron has excited."

"Quite so, sir," Beechey replied. "The dock has been filled with carriages every day. Persons of great eminence come to bid us a good voyage. We can hardly load the ship for all the visitors."

"Let me petition Captain Buchan to move the vessels downriver."

The captain agreed and, after they were moved, fewer people came on board. Soon the loading was done—provisions for two years, including medicine, clothing, food, water, and trading items.

Since Franklin planned to measure variations of the magnetic needle, the presence of electricity in the atmosphere, and the intensity of magnetic force in northern latitudes, valuable instruments went on aboard. He was also to study the weather, the sea, the stars, and as much of navigation as possible.

At last, on April 25, 1818, the sails were loosed and fell in rippling sheets, and the *Dorothea* and *Trent* moved down the Thames River.

"Steady as she goes," shouted the first mate. "Clap on sail and pull up your coats, ye lubbers! We're headed for the North Pole!"

The farther north they sailed, the colder became the weather. Beechey, in his journal, wrote:

". . . snow fell in heavy showers, and several tons' weight of ice accumulated about the sides of the brig, and formed a complete casing to the planks, which received an additional layer at each plunge of the vessel.

"So great indeed was the accumulation about the bows, that we were obliged to cut it away repeatedly with axes, to relieve the bowsprit from the enormous weight that was attached to it; and the ropes were so thickly covered with ice that it was necessary to beat them with large sticks to keep them in a state of readiness . . ."

They crossed the Arctic Circle and now had continual daylight. The sun shone even at midnight, imparting to the ice-choked sea a strange appearance. Off the coast of Spitsbergen, they finally encountered "the pack," a broken mass of ice beyond which they could not pass.

Franklin stood on the quarterdeck of the *Trent,* gazing out over a plain of ice that stretched to the north as far as the eye could see. Off to one side the icy peaks of Spitsbergen rose into the clouded sky. A beautiful sight, he thought. He scanned it with his telescope. Snow-clad valleys lay bleak and white. Great glaciers clung to the barren land—as if they were giant rivers that had forgotten to run.

Franklin and Beechey took a rowboat to explore the coast of this frozen island group. Suddenly an avalanche of ice broke away from a glacier and fell with a grinding crash into the sea. Water flew in all directions, and waves plunged outward, dangerously lifting the small boat. The newly formed iceberg plunged completely out of sight. For a moment nothing could be seen but furiously whirling water and clouds of spray. Then the monstrous mass of ice ponderously rose above the surface, water spilling from it in foaming falls. Moving closer to the awesome sight, Franklin and Beechey guessed that the iceberg was nearly a quarter of a mile around and weighed more than 400,-000 tons.

John Franklin had never seen anything like it. The sight refreshed him. It brought back that excitement of exploration that he had known so well in Australia.

Cold wind plucked his breath away. Glare from the

ice kept burning his eyes. The weight of heavy clothes slowed down his travel. But to John Franklin it was anything but dull.

He saw another iceberg plunging into the sea, and streams of auks flying across the water to their nests in the cliffs. With the telescope he saw the cliffs covered with other birds—especially guillemots, cormorants, and gulls. Ice floating past held sleepy walruses, stretching their bulky forms in the light of the low-lying sun.

Hunters gave chase after ducks and seals, or stalked reindeer on land, supplying the ship with meat. On one occasion the hunters, after having injured several walruses on land, were attacked by them at sea. The walruses snorted with rage and rose in great numbers around the boats, according to Beechey's account of the expedition. It was with the utmost difficulty, he said, that the

Walrus attack, engraved from a drawing by Frederick Beechey. For a portrait of Beechey, see page 223

hunters kept the boat from being upset by the walruses, who placed their tusks upon the gunwales or struck the side of the boat with their heads.

"It was the opinion of our people that in this assault the walruses were led by one animal in particular, a much larger and more formidable beast than any of the others . . . He withstood all the blows of their tomahawks without flinching, and his tough hide resisted the entry of the whale lances, which were unfortunately not very sharp, and soon bent double.

"The horde was so numerous and their attacks so incessant, that there was no time to load a musket, which, indeed, was the only effectual mode of seriously injuring them. The purser, fortunately, had a gun loaded, and the [men] now being nearly exhausted with chopping and sticking at their assailants, he snatched it up and thrusting the muzzle down the throat of the leader, fired into his bowels.

"The wound proved mortal, and the animal fell back amongst his companions, who immediately desisted from the attack, assembled around him, and in a moment quitted the boat, swimming away as hard as they could with their leader, whom they actually bore up with their tusks, and assiduously preserved from sinking . . ."

Now and then the *Dorothea* and the *Trent* sailed out to examine the ice pack. By the first week of July, the great ice mass had sufficiently cracked so that lanes of water opened into the midst of it. The time had come. Summer was passing rapidly. If they were to get on to the North Pole they had to proceed at once.

The two ships sailed into the pack. No sooner had they entered than the movements of wind and water combined to close the passage ahead of them and behind them.

Trapped! Both vessels, surrounded by the pack, lay entirely at the mercy of the weather and the shifting, floating ice. For three weeks they lay as helpless as a ship with a broken mast. They pulled themselves laboriously from one small channel to another, but to no avail. The ice closed in and wedged them tightly.

Once the *Trent* was lifted out of the water by an enormous mass of ice thrusting under her bows. Franklin and the crew watched anxiously, fearful lest the bow be broken.

Ice cracked and ground ominously around them, shoving against the sides of the ships. A bitter storm arose. Outside the pack they heard the wind screaming and the waves crashing against the ice, but here inside they were so perfectly sheltered that there were scarcely any breezes.

With this delay, Captain Buchan knew that they could not go farther north. It was the end of July and summer even now had advanced too far. The sea would soon be freezing solid once again. Worse yet, the ships were bent and twisted by the pressure of the ice.

Tacking the ships this way and that, they finally made their way to the open sea. No sooner was this done than another howling gale blew up, creating waves that furiously struck the little ships. The ice loomed dangerously close and their situation became so perilous that they had only one hope of shelter—to sail back into the pack!

But could they? Huge blocks of ice bobbed in the raging waters. Through the driving rain and snow, Franklin squinted his eyes to find an opening into which they could get the *Trent,* but there was none to see. The pack had closed.

The ship now lay in an extremely dangerous position. As close as she was to the pack, where giant waves crashed into the cliffs of ice, it seemed as if she would strike at any moment. Despite this peril, Franklin issued orders calmly to his officers. Men worked fiercely to keep the ship from careening into the blocks of floating ice. It was no use. In a burst of fury, the gale drove them toward a group of icebergs.

"Each person instinctively secured his own hold," wrote Lieutenant Beechey, "and, with his eyes fixed upon the masts, awaited in breathless anxiety the moment of concussion. It soon arrived; the brig, cutting her way through the light ice, came in violent contact with the main body. In an instant we all lost our footing, the masts bent with the impetus, and the cracking timbers from below bespoke a pressure which was calculated to awaken our serious apprehensions.

"The vessel staggered under the shock . . . The next wave, curling up under her counter, drove her about her own length within the margin of ice, where she gave one roll, and was immediately thrown broadside to the wind by the succeeding wave, which beat furiously against her stern, and brought her lee side in contact with a piece of ice about twice her own dimensions . . .

"Literally tossed from piece to piece, we had nothing left but patiently to abide the issue, for we could scarcely keep our feet, much less render any assistance to the vessel. The motion was so great that the ship's bell, which in the heaviest gale of wind had never struck by itself, now tolled so continually that it was ordered to be muffled."

The sailors clambered over the masts as best they could. They gripped the ice—encrusted lines and held on for their lives, clinging to the rigging lest they be blown into the sea.

Tossed about like a chunk of ice, the little brig at last reached shelter within the pack. Next morning, the storm was gone. Buchan and Franklin sailed their crippled vessels back to Spitsbergen.

In despair, they assessed the damage. The *Trent* had

been badly mauled, and the *Dorothea* was stove in on her port side. It was a wonder that either ship still floated.

Worse yet, the warmth of summer was passing rapidly, and the truth was that they had lost their chance to get to the Pole.

They had also lost another chance to search for the Northwest Passage. But maybe Ross and Parry had found it already.

On July 30, 1818, the expedition was driven furiously into the ice pack by a gale off the coast of Spitsbergen. The ships are shown being perilously tossed by giant waves among the chunks of ice broken from the pack. This engraving was made from a drawing by Frederick Beechey, Franklin's lieutenant aboard the brig *Trent*, shown at extreme left

Eleven

CANADA

Ross and Parry had explored along the broken coast of Baffin Island. Ice had turned them back, but what they saw made them believe that the Northwest Passage had been located.

The search was getting close! With the coming of 1819, two new expeditions were under way—one under Parry in another attempt to enter the Northwest Passage by sea, and one under Franklin to reach the Polar Sea by crossing overland through Canada.

No one could have been more delighted with such a command than the young lieutenant. He and his men would be in Canada and the Arctic for two years, three at the most. Their first destination was the Coppermine River, and down that river they would float in canoes to the Polar Sea and explore along the coast. Somewhere up there was the Northwest Passage. Franklin's orders were to find it.

Yet Canada, he was told, could be a hostile land. In winter, the rivers were frozen solid. The sun often did not shine for weeks and the temperature fell far below zero. In summer the heat would be intense—and nearly always accompanied by the curse of mosquitoes. Food would be scant, roads and trails nearly nonexistent, Indians and traders sometimes unreliable—or even dangerous.

Lieutenant Franklin did not feel the least disturbed by all this. However, he had to do all that he possibly could to equip the expedition to meet such conditions, and to hire the best possible men for it.

This meant expert boatmen to navigate Canadian rivers and lakes and, on his way to Canada, in vessels of the Hudson's Bay Company, Franklin stopped at the village of Stromness, in the Orkney Islands of Scotland. In this village lived skilled fishermen who handled a boat as well as any.

But the Stromness boatmen were very much in demand, for a herring fishery had just been built in the islands. This year five times as many boats and men were needed as last year. The Hudson's Bay Company could not even find enough persons for its own Canadian work.

Despite all this, John Franklin insisted that the local authorities make every effort to recruit men for the voyage. Consequently, a notice was posted on the door of the village church and Franklin was assured that this was the "surest and most direct channel for the conveyance of information" to the boatmen.

On the afternoon of June 16, 1819, two Hudson's Bay Company ships, with Franklin and his crew among the passengers, weighed anchor and sailed from the harbor of Stromness out into the Atlantic Ocean toward Canada. Franklin had wanted eight boatmen. He got four, and even they were reluctant to go. They agreed to accompany the expedition only as far as Fort Chipewyan. That was not far enough.

Franklin stood perplexed at the rail, watching the Orkney Islands disappear in the fog. Fort Chipewyan was scarcely halfway on the route across Canada to the Cop-

Portrait of John Franklin

permine River. If the Stromness men left him at that point, how would he go on? He thought about this and hundreds of other details on the voyage across the Atlantic. Could he hire more men at York Factory, the point of departure on the west coast of Hudson Bay? Would the boats be ready? Were there enough supplies?

As the ships sailed slowly against strong headwinds and heavy seas, Franklin checked and compared his chronometers. He issued a general memorandum for the guidance of his men who, in addition to the Stromness boatmen, included Dr. John Richardson, a surgeon in the Royal Navy and a gentleman scientist; Robert Hood and George Back, both midshipmen and both artists (Back had served under Franklin on the *Trent*); and John Hepburn, a seaman.

A month passed. Toward the end of July they met a whaling ship whose captain reported dangerous icebergs ahead. Two of his vessels, he said, had been entirely crushed between vast masses of ice.

"Were the crews saved?" someone asked.

"Yes, God be praised."

"What of Lieutenant Parry?" Franklin asked anxiously. "Did you see him or his ships, the *Hecla* and *Griper*?"

"Not a sign, Lieutenant," the whaling captain replied. "But the wind has cleared Baffin Bay of ice. That's a good sign."

On toward Canada the two ships sailed, and at the end of July they entered a region of icebergs. Franklin wrote, describing the voyage:

"In the afternoon of the 30th, a very dense fog came on; and about six p.m., when sailing before a fresh breeze, we were suddenly involved in a heavy stream of ice.

"Considerable difficulty was experienced in steering through the narrow channels between the different masses in this foggy weather, and the ship received several severe blows."

Day after day they tacked the ship frequently, barely missing collisions with giant icebergs. On the morning of August 7 they sighted Resolution Island, at the entrance to Hudson Strait. But a dense fog rolled in and the breeze died. The ship, surrounded by loose ice, became helpless.

Desperately they tried to find the direction in which they were drifting. Suddenly, Franklin wrote:

". . . we had the alarming view of a barren rugged shore within a few yards, towering over the mast heads.

"Almost instantly afterwards the ship struck violently on a point of rocks, projecting from the island; and the ship's side was brought so near to the shore, that poles were prepared to push her off.

"This blow displaced the rudder . . . A gentle swell freed the ship from this perilous situation, but the current hurried us along in contact with the rocky shore, and the prospect was most alarming.

"On the outward bow was perceived a rugged and precipitous cliff, whose summit was hid in the fog, and the vessel's head was pointed towards the bottom of a small bay, into which we were

York Factory

rapidly driving. There now seemed to be no probability of escaping shipwreck, being without wind, and having the rudder in its present useless state . . .

"The ship again struck in passing over a ledge of rocks, and happily the blow replaced the rudder, which enabled us to take advantage of a light breeze . . ."

But the ship struck repeatedly. Farther on it slammed against an iceberg that lay partly on shore. Splintering and cracking of the ship's hull could be heard. Women and children rushed on deck.

The officers ordered them to go below, to no avail. Faces turned up toward the masts. If the ship struck much more, the masts would snap.

Another crash. The masts swayed. Franklin thought the strain would break them, but they held. The fog cleared, and the breeze grew stronger. The ship moved away from land, but was leaking badly. A signal of distress was hoisted, whereupon the companion ship took the vessel in tow. Its captain sent carpenters aboard to help repair the leak.

Thus battered, the little vessel sailed across Hudson Bay. At the end of August the ships anchored at the outpost of York Factory, gateway to the interior of Canada.

Twelve

EXPLORING
THE INTERIOR

"Hold that line!"

"Pull it tighter!"

The commands echoed up and down the river and through the deep forest. There was a chill in the September air as the men pulled their big boat upstream. Suddenly one of the men slipped and fell with a splash, breaking the tow rope.

"Catch that rope!"

Offshore, the big boat began to drift free. The steersman leaped into the water. "I'll hold it," he shouted. "Find that rope!"

Another man leaped into the water and swam out in search of the loose rope end.

"Over here!" yelled an Orkney Islander.

"A gauche! A gauche!" shouted one of the French Canadians.

John Franklin strode into the water to steady the boat. "Keep her from going broadside," he said. "Don't let her go loose. She'll break to pieces against those stones."

The other officers of the expedition leaped into the stream to hold the boat steady. It was a York boat, of the kind used by the Hudson's Bay Company to carry furs and other supplies along the streams and across the lakes of Canada. It measured forty feet long, and was sharp at both ends and wide in the middle. Boxes and bundles piled high in it had been covered with canvas and securely lashed.

"Here's the rope," came a shout from downstream.

"Hold the boat, men," Franklin said, "head to the current."

A Canadian carried the line ashore. Once again the men on the bank resumed pulling. The boat moved slowly upriver.

Franklin and his officers climbed out of the water, and moved toward the trail.

It wasn't much of a trail, winding along the edge of the Hayes River, in and out among the spruce and willow. Franklin walked for a while at the rear of the party. The Orkney men "tracked" the boat by pulling it along the bank. They took turns at the rope. They had to. It was tiring work.

Sometimes they stumbled over logs fallen in the path. Sometimes they slipped on wet rocks. Well, thought Franklin, the going would get worse the farther they advanced into the interior of Canada.

He watched the officers ahead. Dr. Richardson, short and stocky with light brown hair, walked rapidly, far in the lead. He usually took the lead, searching, studying, taking notes on all the natural features of interest. Dr. Richardson kept a scientific journal, as Franklin had seen Bauer and Brown do in Australia. Plants, animals, weather, Indians—nothing escaped the doctor. Watching Richardson look here and there, stop for a flower or rock, leap after a frightened deer, Franklin felt relieved. The expedition was in good scientific hands. And good medical hands, too. The doctor was a surgeon in the Navy. If anything went wrong . . .

Franklin was also well pleased with the two midshipmen, George Back and Robert Hood. Both were young and energetic, hard-working, and eager. Back had turned in a fine performance on the *Trent* in their explorations north of Spitsbergen. Both, with an extraordinary talent for drawing, would make a picture record of the expedition. Hood's job was to survey the rivers, take bearings with a pocket compass, estimate distances, and make sketches of scenes along the way.

The other member of the crew, apart from the Orkney Islanders and the Canadians, was John Hepburn, a seaman of many years' experience. Franklin could not remember when he had known a harder worker than Hepburn. Often Franklin and Hepburn talked of the days of Nelson and battles at sea, for Hepburn had also served on a man-o'-war. As the officers' helper of the expedition, Hepburn had as hard a job as any, and Franklin knew it. Hepburn packed supplies, carried equipment, pitched tents, built fires—anything that was demanded of him. Right now he had the lead position on the tow rope, pulling the boat with all his might. Franklin smiled as he watched; men like Hepburn were hard to find.

When they entered the mouth of the Hill River, they were joined by some trading boats. It was now possible to pole their way along the smooth water, but the river was so low that they often had to jump into the water and lift the boat over hidden rocks.

Throughout September the little party trekked southwestward. They fished for trout and carp and sturgeon. They hunted for deer and moose, or watched at sunrise for flocks of geese overhead.

At night they pitched their tents and kindled a fire,

cooked supper and ate it quickly, checked maps, records, and equipment, then crawled exhausted beneath their buffalo robes. Each evening, on maps that he kept in a leather pouch, Hood carefully traced the route of the day. Franklin helped, correcting distances and directions, and comparing them with his record of travel. Franklin also cared for the chronometers, those delicate timekeepers used in finding the longitude of each important landmark along the way.

One night he and Hood and Back and Richardson gathered around the fire to examine their route.

"We are almost at Lake Winnipeg," said Franklin.

"Is this as far south as we go?" Hood asked.

Franklin traced the Saskatchewan River upstream

Flocks of geese and ducks left the water and flew overhead as Franklin's boat moved up the Hill River, accompanied by trading boats. (Engraving from an original drawing by Robert Hood)

past two Hudson's Bay Company posts. "Yes," he replied. "At Cumberland House and Carlton House we shall get men and supplies and turn north."

His finger moved along a narrow line north to Lake Athabasca and Great Slave Lake, then into country marked *unknown*.

"Beyond here," he said, "we know nothing."

Hood looked up. "But Mackenzie . . . and Hearne . . . ?"

Franklin nodded. "I know. They are the only Europeans before us to have beheld the Polar Sea from land." He recalled how Samuel Hearne, of the Hudson's Bay Company, journeyed in 1770 down the Coppermine River to the Polar Sea. The company had hoped he would determine whether that sea were navigable and whether the frozen lands of the north were fur-producing lands.

"I have read Hearne's journal," said Franklin, "and while I do not say that his figures were wholly inaccurate, still I think we have much to do in that region. As to Mackenzie, he traced only the route of the Mackenzie River to its mouth. Between that river and Hudson Bay nearly the entire northern coast is a blank."

Dr. Richardson was thoughtful. The flickering firelight gave his bearded face a somber aspect. "The Canadians were telling me today," he said, "that they hear bad things about the Coppermine River."

"Bad things?"

"They say the Eskimos are dangerous. No white man dares to enter their country."

Franklin rose and put away his maps. "Hearne did," he said. "So shall we. Let's get some sleep."

One morning they awoke to find a heavy fall of snow

covering their blankets. Despite the increasing cold and snow, they paddled, pulled, and poled steadily onward, through storms, around rapids, across bogs. When necessary they unloaded the boat and carried everything over slippery rocks beside roaring rapids and falls.

On the 27th of September, 1819, Franklin wrote:

"We began the ascent of Trout River, and in the course of the day passed three portages and several rapids. At the first of these portages the river falls between two rocks about sixteen feet, and it is necessary to launch the boat over a precipitous rocky bank. This cascade is named the *Trout-Fall,* and the beauty of the scenery afforded a subject for Mr. Hood's pencil."

At another waterfall Franklin wrote in his journal:

"I shall long remember the . . . wildness of the scenery which surrounded these falls; rocks piled on rocks hung in rude and

Rapids on Trout River. This engraving, from a drawing made by Robert Hood, shows how the men of the Franklin expedition portaged around obstacles in their path

shapeless masses over the agitated torrents which swept their bases, whilst the bright and variegated tints of the mosses and lichens that covered the face of the cliffs, contrasting with the dark green of the pines which crowned their summits, added both beauty and grandeur to the scene."

Sometimes they made only a mile in one day, sometimes nearly thirty-five. Each morning they rose before dawn, ate, struck camp, loaded the boat, and resumed their march by the first light of day. Several times the boat got caught broadside in the current and swept against a rock. Having to stop to repair the damage angered Franklin. The sooner they arrived at Cumberland House, he thought, the sooner they would hire their full party and continue to the Polar Sea.

Norway House

One day Franklin slipped on some moss at the edge of the river and fell into the roaring rapids. Plunging from one rocky ledge to another, he clawed at the smooth, water-worn rocks in a desperate effort to regain the bank. Seeing a willow that extended from the bank he fought his way to it, clutched it, and was pulled to shore by two of the Canadians. The chronometer he carried was damaged.

They landed briefly at Norway House, originally built by a colony of Norwegians and now a trading post belonging to the Hudson's Bay Company. Here the chronometer was repaired and on they went.

They hoisted a sail on the boat, sailed around the northern shore of Lake Winnipeg, and entered the Saskatchewan River.

October came, and with it nightly frosts. The weather turned cold and stormy, Franklin wrote, "and we had to contend against a strong head wind. The spray froze as it fell, and the oars were so loaded with ice as to be almost unmanageable."

On the 23rd of October they arrived at Cumberland House, outpost of the Hudson's Bay Company. Now, thought Franklin, they could hire hunters, guides, and interpreters and proceed more rapidly.

"Guides?" said the company agent. "Hunters? Interpreters? I'm sorry, Lieutenant. There are none here to hire."

NOTE: Places on Franklin's route, mentioned in this and the following chapter, are shown on the map on page 122.

Thirteen

WINTER

Cumberland House was located on an island between the Saskatchewan River and Pine Island Lake. Here in a group of buildings constructed of logs, surrounded by high stockades, and flanked with wooden bastions, the North West Company and the Hudson's Bay Company both carried on their trade with the Indians and others who lived and traveled in the North.

The surrounding country was flat and swampy, with small lakes and occasional outcroppings of limestone. Along the banks of the river raspberries grew and aspen, a tree much used at the settlement for firewood. There were larches in the swamps, pines and spruce in the deep forest, and alder around the lakes. Back in the woods were strawberries, cherries, currants, and gooseberries.

But now there were no berries. With the coming of winter, the deciduous trees stood stripped of their leaves. The land lay white and bleak. Only the pines and other evergreens seemed alive. Among them the moose and caribou stepped silently through the deep snow.

Here John Franklin and his men spent the winter of 1819–1820. The river froze over completely, and so low was the temperature that even with fires in their rooms, the men could not keep warm without heavy clothing.

"In going out, however," Franklin wrote, "we never

suffered the slightest inconvenience from the change of temperature, though the thermometer, in the open air, stood occasionally thirty degrees below zero."

In this icy land, Dr. Richardson found more than enough to keep him busy. Around the post came ravens, magpies, partridges, and crossbills. Sometimes a fox or a wolf ventured near the settlement. At night the aurora borealis filled the sky with brilliant color in striking patterns.

When he was not examining aspects of nature, Dr. Richardson studied the lives and customs of the Indians. In this vicinity they were mostly Cree Indians, wretchedly poor and diseased but friendly and peaceful, and the settlement depended upon them for supplies.

In his months at Cumberland House, Dr. Richardson learned how the Crees played games, conducted their family life, hunted, worshiped, tattooed their bodies, held festivals, and raised their young. He learned some of their language, and how they traded and paid for things with beaver skins—the standard of exchange. All these he wrote about in his notebooks, careful to preserve the greatest possible accuracy.

But interesting though the surroundings were, John Franklin knew that waiting would gain them little. The Stromness men had asked Franklin to let them go home, and he did so. Now he was badly in need of help, which he had hoped to hire here. He asked where he could find guides and interpreters since there were none at Cumberland House.

"At Fort Chipewyan," one of the traders informed him.

"Then I will go there," Franklin said, "at once."

"In the middle of January?" the trader asked. "It's near nine hundred miles to the north."

"I have waited long enough," Franklin replied. "If we are to reach the Polar Sea we must arrange for help and do it soon."

The traders shook their heads.

Leaving Richardson and Hood to follow later and join them in the spring, Franklin, Back, and Hepburn set off on foot into the frozen wilderness. Their equipment was loaded onto two dog-drawn carioles (a type of sleigh) and two sledges, whose drivers had been furnished by both of the trading companies.

Their snowshoes were made of light strips of wood fastened at the ends and spread apart by cross-pieces. The spaces between bars were tightly laced with leather thongs, and the front turned up like the prow of a boat. All this was attached to the feet by leather straps around the heel. Although the toe was tied in place, the heel rose free with every step. When the wearer walked, the rear of each snowshoe simply dragged in the snow. Getting accustomed to wearing them was not easy. Each snowshoe was nearly six feet long and one-and-a-half feet wide, and weighed two pounds when free of snow. They were usually clogged with snow, however, and walking all day in them left the feet chafed and blistered, or "galled" as Franklin called it. He wrote:

"The termination of the day's journey was a great relief to me, in consequence of my feet having been galled by the snow-shoes; this, however, is an evil which few escape on their initiation to winter travelling. It excites no pity from the more experienced companions of the journey, who travel on as fast as they can, regardless of your pain."

In the bitter cold, they had to wear heavy and sturdy clothing. Franklin described it thus:

"The general dress of the winter traveller is a *capot,* having a hood to put up under the fur cap in windy weather, or in the woods, to keep the snow from his neck; leathern trowsers [sic] and Indian stockings which are closed at the ankles, round the upper part of his mocasins [sic], or Indian shoes, to prevent the snow from getting into them. Over these he wears a blanket, or leathern coat, which is secured by a belt round his waist, to which his fire-bag, knife, and hatchet are suspended."

They followed each other Indian file, in the track of the leader. So cold was the air that the mercury in the thermometer froze. Franklin tried to obtain a latitude reading, but moisture in the sextant had frozen and rendered the instrument useless. Tea froze in their tin cups before they could drink it.

Camp was no problem. They simply stopped, scraped away the snow, placed some pine branches on the ground, spread out their blankets and coats and slept with a good fire at their feet. Their only other covering was the canopy of stars overhead, and the only sounds were those of wolves howling in the forest.

Snow fell one night and covered them, adding a warm layer to the blankets they already had. Back's buffalo robe caught fire another night and seared his shoes. He leaped up painfully, threw off his blankets, and ran out into the snow until his shoes cooled off again.

A strong and piercing wind blew in their faces as they went on, and they had to rub their flesh to keep it from freezing. By the time they arrived at Carlton House, on the first of February, they were glad to stop for a few days' rest.

At this provision post for Indians and travelers, dried meat and fat were made into a nourishing mixture known

Above: Winter traveling in the Arctic
Below: George Back, who made both drawings, called this "Manner of Making a Resting Place on a Winter's Night, March 15, 1820." Snowshoes were either stuck in a snowbank or hung on a tree

as pemmican. To travelers in the North, this pemmican could be the difference between life and death, when other food was scarce. It was rich. It was easy to carry. Stored in leather bags it kept fresh for long periods of time. Therefore, pemmican became an important food on winter journeys, and at Carlton House the Hudson's Bay Company and the North West Company had each made nearly four hundred bags this year.

One evening an old Cree Indian came to the trading post and told one of the traders: "The Indians are talking of killing all the white people around here this year."

Franklin and Back looked quickly at the trader, whose face did not change. "Is that so?" he asked.

"Yes," the Indian replied. Then, smiling, he added, "Ay! A pretty state we would be in without the goods you bring us."

With a salute of musketry in their honor, Franklin and his party left Carlton House on February 9, 1820, and set out again on the northward trail. They left the Saskatchewan River and, plowing through deep snow that slowed them down, headed north toward Fort Chipewyan, on Lake Athabasca.

By now they had become used to the snowshoes. No longer did they suffer pain from mile after mile of trudging through snow. Passing nameless lakes, Franklin and Back realized that they were getting farther into unknown country. Questions nagged at their minds again and again: would they find help at Fort Chipewyan? Were the Indians friendly? And—far to the north—was Parry succeeding in his attempt by sea to traverse the Northwest Passage?

From Isle à la Crosse Lake they struck out to the

Route of Franklin as described in Chapters 12 and 13

northwest until they reached the Athabasca River and then, on its icy surface, turned directly north again. Once they came upon some Chipewyan Indians, and asked about the country beyond Lake Athabasca. The Indians shook their heads and said: "Eskimo."

After covering 857 miles in two months, the little party arrived at Fort Chipewyan on March 26, 1820. Franklin immediately inquired of the company agent what lay to the north. Snow, came the reply. Ice. Barren ground. Eskimo country. No one goes there.

Franklin frowned. He had supposed that the Canadian *voyageurs*—the Frenchmen—went anywhere. Not so, said the agent. It was unlikely that they could be induced to go north of Slave Lake. Eskimos had already destroyed a party sent to open a trading post.

An interpreter at the fort told them how to reach the Coppermine River and proceed down it to the sea. He sketched on the floor a map of the river and seacoast. "The Copper Indians can give you more information," he said.

Just then an old Chipewyan Indian named Black Meat came in. He saw the map and recognized it immediately. Bending over, he added a path along the seacoast, saying that he had followed this once in returning from a war excursion that his tribe had made against the Eskimos. Was the sea free of ice? Was there a passage? Yes, he replied, at least close to shore.

Franklin next set to work seeking help to take the expedition north. Messengers went out from the post in all directions with news that the English naval officers were hiring guides and hunters. He also ordered the construction of a canoe, specially designed for his purposes. With the coming of April the snow and ice began to melt, and the first birds of spring arrived. By May the first anemone flowers opened, though ice still covered Athabasca Lake.

"There can scarcely be a higher gratification, than . . . witnessing the rapid change which takes place in the course of a few days in the spring; scarcely does the snow disappear from the ground before the trees are clothed with thick foliage, the shrubs open their leaves, and put forth their variegated flowers, and the whole prospect becomes animating. The spaces between the rocky hills, being for the most part swampy, support willows and a few poplar. These spots are the favourite resort of the mosquitoes, which incessantly torment the unfortunate persons who have to pass through them," wrote Franklin.

Franklin hoped to induce the Canadian voyageurs to accompany him, but they asked too much money for going into dangerous territory. He hoped for abundant supplies, but the companies advised that their stores had recently been depleted and they could not give nearly as much as Franklin asked.

With the coming of June mosquitoes swarmed so heavily about the house and tormented the men so incessantly, that they were compelled to keep the rooms constantly filled with smoke, the only way they knew to drive the insects away.

Early in July, their canoe was finished. It measured 32½ feet long and nearly five feet wide. Franklin thought it feeble and slender, but it was the kind of canoe Hearne had recommended—and Hearne was the only European ever to have gone down the Coppermine River. The question was whether this frail canoe could carry their three thousand pounds of equipment.

As the time for departure neared, oarsmen and hunters (some with canoes) began to sign on with the expedition: first six men; then another five; then an interpreter named St. Germain; then Mr. Wentzel, one of the agents of the North West Company; even some Canadian voyageurs. All this gave Franklin more hope than he had had before. But the hope was soon dashed.

Richardson and Hood arrived from Cumberland House on July 13 with news that some of the outposts that had been saving food for Franklin's expedition—food that Richardson had planned to pick up on his way—had suffered such a severe winter that the occupants had eaten it all, or nearly all.

"At one place," Richardson reported, "we got ten bags of pemmican. As soon as we left we found that all of it was moldy. We threw it away."

The prospect of having to commence their journey almost destitute of provisions distressed Franklin greatly. But they had to go on. They could not stay and use up the food of Fort Chipewyan.

Was there ammunition? No, Richardson replied. Spirits? None. Tobacco? A little. Their stores consisted of seventy pounds of moose meat and a little barley—which would not last long. They still had preserved meats and chocolate and soup from England, but that was nearly gone.

They would have to live off the land. Yet how—without ammunition? There were fish in the lakes, to be sure, but how many?

Fourteen

FORT ENTERPRISE

The canoes were loaded on the morning of July 18, 1820, and the party embarked in high spirits from Fort Chipewyan out across the lake. The crews burst into a lively paddling song offshore and their voices broke the stillness of the lake.

In the Slave River they were carried swiftly northward by the current. Many rapids had to be portaged, and two of the canoes once crashed together and broke off a bow, which necessitated a stop for repairs. Storms struck, and the temperature rose to 110 degrees. In this stifling heat, the mosquitoes grew so bad that the explorers were obliged to break up camp and continue their journey down the river at night.

None cursed the mosquitoes more than Hood:

"They swarmed under our blankets, goring us, and steeping our clothes in blood . . . The wound does not swell, like that of the African mosquito, but it is infinitely more painful; and when multiplied an hundred fold, and continued for so many successive days, it becomes an evil of such magnitude, that cold, famine, and every other concomitant of an inhospitable climate, must yield the pre-eminence to it.

"It chases the buffalo to the plains, irritating him to madness; and the reindeer to the seashore, from which they do not return till the scourge has ceased."

Despite all the hardships, none would have wished to be anywhere else. On past Fort Resolution, and across Great Slave Lake, the Canadian voyageurs sang as they paddled, and at night they danced around the campfire.

Ten days after leaving Fort Chipewyan they arrived at Fort Providence, a trading post on the northern arm of Great Slave Lake. Here they held long conversations with the Indians and, eventually, after proper ceremony, hired a group of them to go along. They were to be chiefly hunters, supplying the party with food on the northward journey.

Fort Providence was the final trading post before they plunged into the unknown, so they gathered as much provision as they could. Men moved everywhere packing the canoes. Two barrels of gunpowder and 140 pounds of ball and smallshot went aboard. Old guns were wrapped in canvas and stowed away. In one box they packed eight pistols, twenty-four Indian daggers, and knives, chisels, axes, nails, and fastenings for the boats.

As gifts for the Indians they took along blankets, needles, mirrors, beads, and various sizes of fishing nets. Franklin was still uneasy about the food. Although they had some flour, moose meat, pemmican, chocolate, reindeer tongues, and tea, it was not enough.

By the time they left Fort Providence the expedition consisted of Franklin and his officers, Mr. Wentzel, the clerk of the North West Company, seventeen Canadian voyageurs, and three interpreters. There were also three women, wives of the Canadians, who had been brought along to make shoes and clothes for the men wherever their winter post would be set up.

"On the afternoon of the 2d of August," Franklin wrote, "we

commenced our journey, having, in addition to our three canoes, a smaller one to convey the women; we were all in high spirits, being heartily glad that the time had at length arrived when our course was to be directed towards the Coppermine River, and through a line of country which had not been previously visited by any European."

At the mouth of the Yellowknife River they met the Indians whom they had engaged to accompany them.

"This party was quickly in motion after our arrival," Franklin wrote, "and we were soon surrounded by a fleet of seventeen Indian canoes. In company with them we paddled up the river, which is one hundred and fifty yards wide . . . We next crossed a dilatation of the river, about six miles in length, upon which the name of Lake Prosperous was bestowed. Its shores, though scantily supplied with wood, are very picturesque."

It was a noisy party. Quarrels broke out in the Indian canoes, and some of the Indians had to settle these arguments with a paddle. Portage after portage, lake after lake, the party moved on. Animals were scarce. So were fish. "We do not get enough to eat," complained the voyageurs. "How can we work so hard all day, and get so little food?"

Franklin issued some of the preserved meat, and soon this was gone.

Portages were the hardest work. Each box of supplies was taken from the canoes and carried across sharp rocks or into muddy swamps. Sometimes they took all day to cover less than a mile.

With the coming of September, the Indians came to Franklin and said that they could go no farther. The leaves had begun to fall, the days grew colder, and geese

Franklin's party crossing Lake Prosperous accompanied by Indians. (Engraving from original drawing by Hood)

had started flying to the south. Winter would set in soon, they said, and camp would have to be made.

Impatient as Franklin was to get to the Coppermine River, by now not far away, he decided to stop. He knew that they could not go on without the Indians. So on a wooded promontory above the river the men of the expedition, under command of Mr. Wentzel, began to build a winter encampment, while the Indians went out hunting in order to store food for the winter. Franklin sent Back and Hood on an excursion toward the Coppermine River. He and Richardson walked overland in another direction to investigate the upper reaches of that river.

By the time they returned, Wentzel and his men had made good progress in the construction of a fort. The first building was a log one, fifty feet long, and twenty-four wide, divided into a hall, three bedrooms, and a kitchen. The walls and roof were plastered with clay, the floor was laid with roughly hewn planks, and the windows were closed with a parchment of deerskin.

The clay froze as it was daubed on. Later it cracked, and the wind whistled through the walls. Still, Franklin said, it was more comfortable than tents. The Canadians made beds, chairs, and tables to furnish the building, and as hunting expeditions laid in stores for the winter, another house was added and a storehouse for provisions.

To the fort thus established, they gave the name Fort Enterprise, and there they spent the winter of 1820–1821.

As hunting and fishing ended, bitter cold set in. On one occasion the thermometer fell to 57 degrees below zero outside, and forty below inside. Observations were

Fort Enterprise (on hill, at right) above Yellow-Knife River (in the distance at center). (Engraving from original drawing by George Back)

hampered by frost, and even the chronometers stopped. The sun, low and reddish on the southern horizon, rose at eleven in the morning and set at two in the afternoon.

No one can say that it was an idle winter in this tiny camp sealed off from the world. The men engaged in reading, writing, and talking. They often tried to guess what was going on in the rest of the world. News of the death of King George III had arrived, and they wondered how this would affect the future of England.

There were games and singing and dancing, or the making of candles and soap, or the gathering of wood. Sometimes they hiked along the river. Sledding down the embankments was enjoyed by all. The officers corrected charts, completed drawings, and wrote descriptions of the aurora borealis. Dr. Richardson, even in the depth of winter, collected lichens from beneath the snow and carefully made descriptions of them. On Sundays, religious services were conducted in French and English.

Now and then a few supplies arrived, but not enough to allow the party more than a single meal a day. To Franklin, the lack of provisions became so serious that he dispatched Midshipman Back to Fort Chipewyan to arrange for supplies to be sent in the spring.

Back's journeys that winter covered a distance of 1,100 miles—on snowshoes. His only cover at night was a single blanket and a deerskin. Frequently he was without food for two or three days at a time. By March he had returned, and from Fort Chipewyan later came a few additions to the larder. There was nothing else to be had.

Once more the robins came, and the hour for departure approached. And once again, the Indians balked. Only after hours of pleading and coaxing could they be induced to stay with the expedition as hunters.

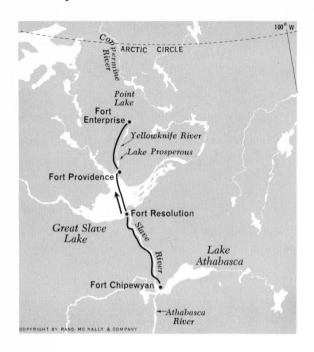

Franklin's route, described above

June brought constant daylight, and the voyageurs set off in happy spirits. The others traveled by canoe and sledge. In a short time they were spread out across the frozen surface of Point Lake.

A cold and icy gale struck them. At one point Franklin fell through the ice into the lake, but was rescued without injury. The same thing happened to Back and others.

Soon they crossed the Arctic Circle. On the barren hills around them, trees were twisted and stunted, mostly in protected places. This meant that little wood was available for fires and so the explorers used for fuel whatever moss they could find. Some of the Indians deserted the party and went back south. The food supply diminished. Mosquitoes swarmed in great clouds. Broken ice and sharp rocks tore their shoes and cut the feet of the dogs which, as Franklin said, "marked their path with their blood."

But at last they came to the Coppermine River—a roaring, rushing stream—and set their canoes upon it. Away they went, through the water, across still-frozen lakes, past sandy plains and naked, desolate mountains. Franklin was sure of one thing—the rapidity of the river and numerous rapids meant that it would be difficult to navigate upstream, on the return trip. They would have to find some other way back to Fort Enterprise.

Franklin asked the guides how the Coppermine River got its name, and was told that copper in large pieces had been found in every part of this range. The Eskimos often came in search of it. Copper Indians used to come every year to make their weapons and utensils of copper, but not any more. Nowadays they bought those things at the trading posts.

The expedition had entered Eskimo country. The guides warned against lighting fires, and against traveling along ridge-tops where a man could be easily discovered. Watch was kept day and night, and the men slept beside their weapons.

After supper one evening, Dr. Richardson climbed a hill about three miles from the encampment. They watched his small figure as it arrived at the top, then saw him wave his arms excitedly.

"He's seen the Eskimos!" someone shouted.

"No," Franklin said, grabbing his gun and reaching for his snowshoes. "Something more than that, my mates."

"What, sir?"

"He's discovered the sea."

Fifteen

THE POLAR SEA

Paddling quietly, the Canadians steered the canoes across the water. They kept intensive watch, for now the water was very shallow. At last they nudged the canoes against a gravelly bank and stepped out. Not far away, seals cavorted at the mouth of the river.

John Franklin walked along the edge of the Coppermine River and looked across the sea to the north. A chain of islands, appearing solidly frozen in ice, lay off to the northeast. Between the edge of the ice and the mainland directly to the east could be seen a channel of clear, green water. As he watched, compelled by the beauty of the scene, he heard the sound of angry voices.

"Lieutenant Franklin!" It was St. Germain, the interpreter. "The men are terrified. They ask if you intend to go east through that channel."

"Tell them yes."

"They ask in two bark canoes?"

"That is correct."

St. Germain turned and relayed the information to the Canadian voyageurs. He was met by a shaking of heads. To Franklin he said: "They are turning back. They say the journey is too long. The waves are too high for canoes. We will not have enough to eat, especially with the Indian hunters due to leave us now. We do not see wood for fires. If you go that way you will have to return to Fort Enterprise over the barren grounds."

"And you, St. Germain?" Franklin asked, quietly. "Are you a woman, too?"

The interpreter bit his lip. "I am not a fool, Lieutenant. I would go back with the rest of them."

"Listen to me." Franklin's voice was a trifle louder now. "The time we have is short. It cannot be spent in arguing. You—all of you—made a solemn agreement to accompany the expedition. I cannot listen to your pleas for return. Mr. Back, instruct the men to prepare the canoes for departure."

When this was done, and the men had departed, scowling and grumbling, Franklin called the interpreter back. "The Indians are returning to Fort Enterprise. I want you to explain to them more clearly than you have ever explained anything that they are to deposit food and supplies at Fort Enterprise for our return."

"I will, sir."

"I repeat. When we return to Fort Enterprise in a month or two, we *must* have food. Our supplies will be entirely gone. I instruct you to impress this on them until the moment they leave. Do you understand?"

"I do, Lieutenant."

After the departure of the Indians, the party consisted of twenty persons. From that moment on, Franklin and his officers kept careful watch over the Canadians. "I heard that they planned to escape," Hood whispered just after the Indians had gone.

"I am not surprised," said Franklin. "But now with the Indians departed, they dare not leave us—not while we are in Eskimo country."

In loading the canoes they discovered that one of the

bags of shot was missing. Back later learned that the Canadians had secretly distributed it among themselves so that, if the party ran out of food, they could shoot some geese and ducks and not have to share them with the officers.

"How is our food supply?" asked Franklin.

"We have enough for fifteen days," said Hood.

On July 21, 1821, they moved away from shore and paddled eastward along the coast, inside a range of crowded islands. The Englishmen must have felt a great relief in being at sea again, but in these frail canoes . . .

At first they encountered little ice, but bright reflections in the sky told them that plenty of it lay ahead. The sea was open at least; that was exactly what they wanted to learn. But for how far was it open? And how long would it remain unfrozen?

View of the Arctic Sea from the mouth of the Coppermine River. Back's drawing shows the tents and flags of the expedition. At this time (midnight, July 20, 1821), there were 24 hours of daylight

Franklin kept a log, and as they passed new features he named them one by one. An unknown river became Richardson's River. A conspicuous headland became Cape Hearne, in honor of the previous explorer. Lawford Islands were named for his captain on the *Polyphemus* at Copenhagen. Nor did he forget his other captains—Flinders and Buchan.

Soon the fears of the Canadians disappeared. "This evening," Franklin recorded, "we were in high glee at the progress we had made; the disappearance of the ice, the continuance of the land in an eastern direction, and our future prospects formed an enlivening subject of conversation."

But it was not to last. Going on under sail, they came to drift ice, and had to push their canoes through narrow channels in it. If they encountered more ice, if their canoes and equipment should be crushed and lost—Franklin shuddered at the thought. How would they find their way back without the instruments? How could they hunt for food without guns or ammunition? He tried not to think of it. He certainly never mentioned such concerns to the men. They were probably thinking the same things anyway. In situations such as this it was Franklin's nature to pray for the help of Providence to see them through.

Each day, each hour, brought new discovery to them. They had not the slightest idea where the land would lead. Franklin wondered whether he might better have turned to the west from the Coppermine River instead of to the east. Would he ever know?

Geese and ducks flew over the coast. Now and then a deer was seen at the edge of land. Then came ice . . . and more ice. Rain fell. Fog obscured the way. They hugged the land as closely as possible, but sometimes had to cross an open bay. When they did this in the fog, it was always a profound relief to arrive at the other side.

On day in a storm they became surrounded by the ice. Franklin described it.

"Just as we were endeavouring to double a bold cape, the fog partially cleared away, and allowed us an imperfect view of a chain of islands on the outside, and of much heavy ice which was pressing down upon us.

"The coast near us was so steep and rugged that no landing of the cargoes could be effected, and we were preserved only by some men jumping on the rocks, and thrusting the ice off with poles.

"There was no alternative but to continue along this dreary shore, seeking a channel between the different masses of ice which had accumulated at the various points. In this operation both the canoes were in imminent danger of being crushed by the ice, which was now tossed about by the waves that the gale had excited . . ."

The next day, just as they feared, one of the canoes became surrounded. Giant pieces of ice, crowding and grinding together in the wind and current, banged against the fragile craft. Just when they feared the worst, an opening appeared and they quickly paddled to safety.

On they went, sketching and mapping, landing, camping, sending the hunters out. Now and then the hunters returned with a deer or bear or musk-ox, and their food supply was extended a little. A few fish were caught in nets, but never enough for twenty hard-working men, and Franklin knew that they could not sail on much farther.

August came. Cold squalls blew in from the sea, and the wind on one occasion overturned their tents. Driftwood, or any wood, was scarce and they could not often build a fire. That meant they couldn't cook. To make matters worse, they discovered that two of their bags of pemmican had spoiled.

They passed a large river, which they named Hood's River, and found the remains of Eskimo camps, but saw no Indians. A familiar enemy plagued them, even at the edge of the Polar Sea: mosquitoes, piercing, sucking.

Despite these torments, and despite the ice, bad weather, and waves that terrified the voyageurs, they guided their pitching canoes among the islands, charting the land and sea. They had earlier named Coronation Gulf and Arctic Sound. They penetrated deep into Bathurst Inlet and around the eastern side of the Gulf to Buchan's Bay and Cape Flinders. They examined and named peninsulas, headlands, rivers, bays, and islands. Under the circumstances, and considering how small and light their canoes were, it is a wonder they saw as much as they did. Altogether, they paddled and sailed along some 550 miles of the coast of the Polar Sea.

One evening, Franklin called the officers together. "The men are getting more restless than usual," he said.

"Yes," said Hood, "they talk of danger all day."

"What bothers them most is the coming of winter," Back added. "They fear that already it is too late, that we'll starve on our return across the barren grounds to Fort Enterprise."

Franklin's eyes seemed far away. "From the start I have entertained the hope that we would get to Repulse Bay, and that we would meet with Parry. It is not to be God's will." He paused and said: "After striking the rocks repeatedly the canoes are broken and getting weaker. They cannot last much longer."

A gust of icy wind stirred the fire and sent a flurry of

Expedition landing in a storm on the Arctic coast of Canada, August 23, 1821. (Engraving from a drawing by George Back)

sparks into the night air. "The winds rise," Franklin continued. "The season is breaking up. We have provision for three days, and scant chance of finding food the longer we stay." Again he fell silent. The men looked at him. Weariness and disappointment could plainly be seen on his face. When he spoke it was in a tone that was scarcely audible. "Gentlemen," he said, "we must return."

The spirits of the Canadians leaped when they heard the news, and the following night they talked and joked around the fire. Off to one side, John Franklin sat with journal in hand and looked out across the Polar Sea. For a long time he made no movement. Then he began to write:

"When the many perplexing incidents which occurred during the survey of the coast are considered . . . I trust it will be judged that we prosecuted the enterprise as far as was prudent, and abandoned it only under a well-founded conviction that a further advance would endanger the lives of the whole party, and prevent the knowledge of what had been done from reaching England . . .

"Our researches, as far as they have gone, favour the opinion of those who contend for the practicability of a Northwest Passage. The general line of coast probably runs east and west, nearly in the latitude assigned to Mackenzie's River, the Sound into which Kotzebue entered, and Repulse Bay; and I think there is little doubt of a continued sea, in or about that line of direction."

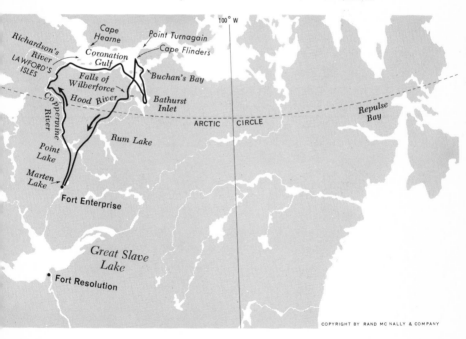

Route of Franklin, described in Chapters 15 and 16. The geography of this region was unknown to Franklin in 1820. He called it the Polar Sea

Sixteen

STARVATION

"August 26, 1821. Previous to our departure this morning an assortment of iron materials, beads, looking-glasses, and other articles were put up in a conspicuous situation for the Eskimos, and the English Union was planted on the loftiest sand-hill, where it might be seen by any ships passing in the offing.

"Here also, was deposited in a tin box, a letter containing an outline of our proceedings, the latitude and longitude of the principal places, and the course we intended to pursue toward Slave Lake.

"Embarking at eight a.m. we proceeded up the river which is full of sandy shoals, but sufficiently deep for canoes in the channels."

These conditions did not last, however, for soon Hood's River became a series of rapids and high waterfalls. As a result, the party was forced to walk.

It was not easy. They carried hatchets, ammunition, nets, ice chisels, instruments, clothing, blankets, and kettles. For the overland journey, two lighter canoes had been constructed from the larger ones, and each of these canoes was carried by one man. Altogether, every man carried about ninety pounds.

The journey was not without its scenic grandeur. Seven miles upstream they came to a roaring waterfall.

"We encamped at the lower end of a narrow chasm," Franklin wrote, "through which the river flows . . . The walls of this chasm are upwards of two hundred feet high, quite perpendicular, and in some places only a few yards apart. The river precipitates itself into it over a rock, forming two magnificent and picturesque falls close to each other. The upper fall is about sixty feet high, and the lower one at least one hundred; but perhaps considerably more, for the narrowness of the chasm into which it fell prevented us from seeing its bottom, and we could merely discern the top of the spray far beneath our feet. The lower fall is divided into two, by an insulated column of rock which

Wilberforce Falls, from George Back's drawing

rises about forty feet above it. The whole descent of the river at this place probably exceeds two hundred and fifty feet . . . I have named these magnificent cascades 'Wilberforce Falls,' as a tribute of my respect for that distinguished philanthropist and Christian. Messrs. Back and Hood took beautiful sketches . . ."

Hardly had they started again when storms attacked. A squall one midnight tore away their tent and drenched them all with rain before they could get it up again. Snow fell on the first of September, filling them with anxiety.

Finding that Hood's River lay too much to the west,

Franklin decided to leave the river and strike out across the barren hills and valleys straight south toward Fort Enterprise. Although from time to time they were able to shoot a hare or partridge, each animal did not go far among twenty hungry men. About this time, the last of their pemmican was issued.

Again the weather worsened. Heavy rain began one night at midnight and poured incessantly until dawn, when it turned to snow. A violent gale swept down upon the little tents.

"As we had nothing to eat," wrote Franklin, the wind howling furiously outside, "and were destitute of the means of making a fire, we remained in our beds all the day; but the covering of our blankets was insufficient to prevent us from feeling the severity of the frost, and suffering inconvenience from the drifting of the snow into our tents.

"There was no abatement of the storm next day; our tents were completely frozen, and the snow had drifted around them to a depth of three feet, and even in the inside there was a covering of several inches on our blankets.

"Our suffering from cold, in a comfortless canvass tent in such weather, with the temperature at $20°$, and without fire, will easily be imagined; it was, however, less than that which we felt from hunger."

Next day they tore their tents from the icy snow and trudged ahead. The wind raged furiously across the land. Those men assigned to carry the canoes were time after time blown down, and on one occasion a canoe crashed to the rocks so violently that it was shattered beyond repair.

How much this accident would delay them in crossing lakes and streams, no one could say. The deed was done. And what would they do with the broken canoe?

"Why, make a fire with it," Franklin said, "and we shall have the last of our portable soup!"

Walking in deep snow exhausted them. The Canadian voyageurs took turns in leading the party and breaking trail. Hood was usually next, watching his compass, keeping track of the direction in which they were traveling. Any mistake in navigation would result in their missing Fort Enterprise, an event that would almost certainly mean disaster.

They came to more hill country, strewn with great boulders on which grew a strange-looking, leathery plant that clung to the rock or peeled away in uneven layers. It was a species of lichen, said Dr. Richardson, called *Gyrophora*. Because of its resemblance to tripe, the stomach wall of cattle, the French Canadians had called it *tripe de roche,* rock tripe.

They dug up a few willows from beneath the snow, built a small fire, and made a stew of the *tripe de roche.* As soon as he tasted it, Hood coughed and spat.

"Ugh!" he said, retching. "My stomach will not accept this!"

Sometimes they supplemented their diet with hares or partridges, or a musk ox, or berries, but everything was scarce—except the *tripe de roche.*

Each river they met was a major obstacle. They had to walk upstream or down as far as they could to find the narrowest place, and sometimes crossed on rocks that were slippery and covered by the strongly flowing current. They slipped and fell into the icy water, getting thoroughly drenched. "We were all wet to the middle," Franklin wrote one night, "our clothes became stiff with the frost, and we walked with much pain for the remainder of the day."

The men grew weaker and the going more hazardous. If anyone broke a leg, thought Franklin, his fate would be sad indeed. No one could carry him. No one could remain behind with him.

At noon on September 10 they sighted a herd of musk-oxen grazing in a valley below. Franklin described it:

"The party instantly halted, and the best hunters were sent out; they approached the animals with the utmost caution, no less than two hours being consumed before they got within gun-shot.

"In the meantime we beheld their proceedings with extreme anxiety, and many secret prayers were, doubtless, offered up for their success. At length they opened their fire, and we had the satisfaction of seeing one of the largest cows fall . . .

"This success infused spirit into our starving party. To skin and cut up the animal was the work of a few minutes. The contents of its stomach were devoured upon the spot, and the raw intestines, which were next attacked, were pronounced by the most delicate amongst us to be excellent."

Several days later they came to a river about 300 yards wide that flowed with a powerful current through a rocky defile. Franklin climbed into the canoe with St. Germain, the interpreter, and Belanger, one of the voyageurs.

They pushed away from shore, but in the wind the heavily laden canoe lost balance and upset, dumping them and their supplies into the icy water. They clung to the canoe and floated along until their feet touched rock.

They emptied the water out of the canoe and righted it. Franklin and St. Germain clambered aboard. Belanger, however, could not climb up; were he to let go of the canoe it would slide away in the rapids before he could get aboard.

Franklin and St. Germain immediately decided to go ashore so that one could return to rescue the Canadian. Accordingly, they hurried down the rapid but struck again. The canoe upset and spilled them into the river. Quickly they regained their footing, righted the canoe, and managed to get back in.

Belanger, immersed to his waist in near-freezing water, his soaked torso exposed to a breeze that was close to zero, called plaintively for help.

When they reached the far shore, Franklin leaped out and St. Germain paddled back as fast as he could. But again the canoe got caught by the current. St. Germain became numbed, and another voyageur took the canoe out. He also failed.

A line was sent out to Belanger, but this attempt also failed. By now, Belanger was weakening, for life ebbs rapidly in icy waters. Finally the canoe reached him, with a rope attached, and the men aboard dragged the now-unconscious Canadian through the water to shore.

Dr. Richardson ordered the frozen man stripped and rolled in blankets. Two men undressed and quickly rolled themselves into the blankets on each side of him.

All this time Franklin watched helplessly on the opposite shore. He paced back and forth, unmindful of his own frozen clothes. Had the canoe been lost, he thought, and the party thus separated, it would have been the doom of them all. As it was, Franklin's journal had plunged overboard and floated away. With it went his observations and every note he had written since leaving Fort Enterprise. (Later, he would rewrite his journal from notes made by Back and Richardson.)

Several hours later Belanger regained his warmth and feeling, and the next day was able to move again. The

Preparing an ecampment on the Barren Grounds, September 16, 1821. (Engraving from a drawing by Back)

entire party succeeded in crossing the river and the journey continued.

South of Rum Lake, their daily fare grew more and more meager, and on some days they had not a thing to eat. In the evening, upon making camp, their first task was to hunt wood and build a fire. They then thawed their frozen shoes. The officers wrote notes of the day's happenings, and prayers were read. Supper, such as it was, usually had to be consumed in the dark. Then, in the blankets, the men dared not pull off their clothes lest they freeze so hard as to be unfit to wear on the morrow.

The voyageurs became irritable, and threatened to throw away their bundles and go on ahead. Franklin knew that they would probably have done so long ago—had they known what track to pursue.

At last, the thing Franklin dreaded happened. One of

the voyageurs, separated from the party while carrying the canoe, fell and broke it to pieces. Little else could have distressed Franklin more, but the voyageurs were delighted. Now they would have less to carry.

The folly of their feelings was soon to be apparent.

The travelers had now gone so long without food that they were reduced to eating parts of old shoes and scraps of leather. One morning they discovered the carcass of a deer that had months before fallen into a cleft of rock. The meat was putrid, but this did not stop the starving explorers. They happily devoured their find—antlers, hoofs, and all.

It was almost October when they arrived at a point on the Coppermine River just upstream from Point Lake. The only way to cross was to build a raft. This they did, though with great difficulty. They fashioned it of green willow sticks lashed together. Since fresh wood was all they had, the raft was not very buoyant and held little more than one man at a time.

Two of the strongest Canadians attempted, against the current and wind, to take the raft across, hoping to get a line to the other side. They failed for lack of paddles.

Tent poles were tied together, but even with this they could not pole their way across. The river was too deep. Again and again, attempts were made to cross, each no more successful than the one before.

"It is hopeless," said one.

"We'll never get the raft across," said another.

Dr. Richardson stepped forward. "I have a plan," said he. "Hand me that rope. I shall swim across with the line, then you can attach the raft and I shall pull it over."

"Swim?" Back asked. "The temperature of that water is 38 degrees!"

The doctor replied: "We cannot stay here all winter." With that he tied the rope around his waist and strode into the river.

The men all gathered at the edge and breathlessly watched as Richardson moved into deeper water and finally started swimming. Before long his arms became so numb that he lost the strength to move them. He turned on his back and, thrashing his legs as violently as he could, approached the opposite bank. At that moment his legs also failed and he sank out of sight.

"Pull!" Franklin shouted to the voyageurs. "Pull the rope!"

Instantly they hauled back on the line and Richardson came again to the surface. Quickly they hauled him back through the water and drew him ashore.

"He's dead," said Hood.

"Not yet," Franklin said. "Get his clothes off."

They stripped away his freezing clothes, revealing a frame that had been so shrunken by hunger that they all caught their breath on seeing it. The Doctor seemed like a skeleton.

"*Que nous sommes maigres!*" the Canadians exclaimed. "How thin we all are!"

A flicker of life showed in the doctor's face. Then he spoke in a whisper, barely loud enough to be heard, and gave them directions. They placed him close to the fire (so close that one side was later almost paralyzed). And not until afterward did they discover that at the moment he had stepped into the water his foot struck an Indian dagger, which cut him to the bone.

Next day, they gathered new materials and made a more buoyant raft. With this they succeeded at last in reaching the other side and continuing their journey.

October came. By now, weak and exhausted and frail as they were, it was all they could do to walk. Hood was weakest, because the *tripe de roche* upset his stomach.

"Back was so feeble as to require the support of a stick in walking," Franklin wrote; "and Dr. Richardson had lameness added to weakness . . . The sensation of hunger was no longer felt by any of us, yet we were scarcely able to converse upon any other subject than the pleasures of eating."

The officers, now unable to gather *tripe de roche,* depended upon Hepburn to collect it, for he somehow retained his strength.

"Don't worry," Franklin would tell them. "We are not far from Fort Enterprise. The Indians will have a cache of food there for us. Our troubles are almost over."

He soon sent Back and St. Germain and three of the voyageurs ahead to find the Indians and add to the supply of food at Fort Enterprise.

Franklin himself now found it necessary to walk at the head of the party so that he could stop the forward men and allow the stragglers to catch up. Otherwise, the impatient voyageurs would have left the party and gone ahead.

Bit by bit they had discarded instruments, books, and other equipment which they became too feeble to carry. By now, their old shoes had been eaten. Nothing remained.

Two of the voyageurs fell in the snow, and Dr. Richardson limped back to help. It was no use. The men could not even speak. The party halted and held a council. Not one of the men was able to return and help the fallen Canadians. It was all each could do to propel himself along. Again the voyageurs pleaded to be allowed to

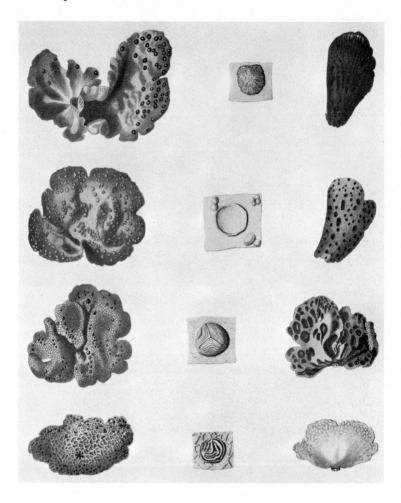

Four species of tripe de roche, or *Gyrophora,* described by Franklin as: *(top) G. muhlenbergii; (second) G. penn-sylvanica; (third) G. hyperborea; (bottom) G. probos-cidea.* The left column shows the general nature of the whole plant; the center column shows the tiny spore cases on each surface; and the right column gives a closer view of parts of the leaf-like structure throw down their packs and push ahead. Hood was nearly incapable of going another step. The constant wading through snow had exhausted them all.

Belanger, no doubt still suffering from his long exposure in the icy waters of the stream, fell against Franklin and burst into tears. "I cannot go on!" he sobbed. "Let me stay . . . Let me stay . . ."

That night they did not even find any *tripe de roche*. Too weak to raise the tent poles, they spent the night under the open sky. With only one blanket and no warm flesh to cover their bones, they had little sleep.

Franklin finally relented and agreed that some of the party could remain behind. None knew how painful this decision was to him. For thousands of miles through the Arctic he had kept his men together. Now, in distress, he was forced to abandon and leave behind the sick and the weak. He wrote:

"I cannot describe my anguish on the occasion of separating. There was, however, no alternative . . . The party was now reduced to five persons, Adam, Peltier, Benoit, Samandre, and myself . . .

"Next morning the breeze was light and the weather mild, which enabled us to collect some *tripe de roche,* and to enjoy the only meal we had had for four days. We derived great benefit from it, and walked with considerably more ease than yesterday. Without the strength it supplied, we should certainly have been unable to oppose the strong breeze we met in the afternoon.

"After walking about five miles, we came upon the borders of Marten Lake, and were rejoiced to find it frozen, so that we could continue our course straight for Fort Enterprise."

As they stumbled and staggered that last few yards up the trail toward the crude log buildings from which they had departed four months before, each man must have felt overwhelmed with excitement—and expectation.

Now, Franklin thought, they could eat their fill; they could take food back to their comrades fallen by the trail. They could . . .

He stopped. The Canadians, coming up, saw him gazing toward the fort, an emptiness in his eyes.

"You have seen something?" Peltier asked.

When Franklin spoke, it was in a whisper. "Do you see any sign of life?"

They squinted their eyes against the glare of the snow.

"Any smoke?" Franklin asked. He stumbled forward. "There should be smoke! They should have a fire!"

Moving as fast as his legs could carry him, he crossed the last steps to the log building and burst through the door. The Canadians followed.

Inside they found the building desolate and empty. There was no trace of the Indians, no sign of food, no letter of directions from Mr. Wentzel, not a single sign-of habitation or supplies. The wind whistled mournfully through the windows, where only shreds of the parchment covering remained. In the darkness they made out a pile of ashes in one corner. In another lay a pile of old deer hides. That was all.

The Canadians fell to the floor, wailing in anguish. Tears rolled down their bearded faces. Franklin, trembling, poked around in the deserted rooms and found a note from Back, who had left just two days before. He was going on with St. Germain, he said, to a place where they might find Indians. If he did not find them at that place, then he would start on to Fort Providence and send help from there. However, he added, he doubted whether any of them could get to Fort Providence without food.

Franklin put down the letter. Even if Back succeeded, it would take too long. By the time help arrived from as far away as Fort Providence, they and their companions on the trail would have perished.

After a while he returned to the Canadians and said: "We are better off than our friends back of us. They have only a tent. We at least have a room. Let us make the best of it. See those old deer hides? Peltier, let us singe them and have a feast. Adam, dig in those ashes for bits of bone and antler. We must carry on as best we can."

Slowly and weakly, they set to work. The temperature stood between ten and fifteen degrees below zero. To keep out some of the cold they covered the windows with boards. Wood was collected, though each man could carry only an armful before sinking in exhaustion beside the tiny fire in the room.

"We procured fuel by pulling up the flooring of the other rooms, and water for cooking, by melting the snow, Franklin said in his journal.

Next morning his body and limbs were so badly swollen that he was able to walk no more than a few steps. Adam was worse, but the others gathered some wood and a little *tripe de roche*. The wind howled and snow drifted around and through the building.

On October 4, a voyageur arrived with a note from Back saying that no Indians had been found. The voyageur himself was almost speechless. He had fallen into a rapid and was covered with ice. Not until they rubbed him, changed his clothes, and gave him some warm bone soup, did he revive.

When two of the other Canadians who had gone with Back returned, Franklin decided to go with them and catch up to Back. He was aware that his clothes had become so badly torn that they scarcely kept out wind and snow. His companions offered to trade clothes with him. With the borrowed clothing and patched shoes, he set out to the south with the two Canadians.

All went well—if slowly—until the second morning, when Franklin fell between two rocks and broke his snow-shoes. Without snowshoes he could not keep up with his fellow travelers. The only course, he knew, was to return.

Before they parted, he wrote a letter to Back, instructing him to send whatever meat he could by the fastest possible means. Then he bade the Canadians bon voyage and returned to Fort Enterprise.

"We perceived our strength decline every day," he wrote, "and every exertion began to be irksome. When we were once seated, the greatest effort was necessary in order to rise, and we had frequently to lift each other from our seats . . .

"We endeavoured to pick some *tripe de roche,* but in vain, as it was entirely frozen . . . We saw a herd of reindeer sporting on the river, about half a mile from the house; they remained there a long time, but none of the party felt themselves strong enough to go after them, nor was there one of us who could have fired a gun without resting it."

One evening Dr. Richardson and Hepburn arrived. They were greeted with embraces and much joy. As soon as Franklin could get the doctor out of earshot from the others he asked about Hood.

A feeling of pain showed on Richardson's face. "He's dead."

Franklin closed his eyes and lowered his head. In a hoarse voice he asked: "And Michel, the Canadian?"

"Also dead," the Doctor replied.

"And Vaillant? Fontano? Perrault?"

"All of them."

"What happened?"

Richardson turned his head. "It is a long story. Let us talk of it tomorrow. See over there—Hepburn has a surprise for us all."

Hepburn had shot a partridge that day. Richardson tore off the feathers and, after holding it over the fire for a few minutes, divided it into six portions. They devoured their shares ravenously—the first fresh meat they had had in thirty-one days.

The following day, Richardson told Franklin what had happened along the trail. "At the stopping place, you will recall, Michel and Hood and I were alone."

"I remember."

"As you know, Hood was very weak. His sight had begun to fail and he endured periods of extreme dizziness. Michel went away for a while and on returning reported that he had chased some deer and found a dead wolf. He gave us some meat, so we believed him."

"Had he seen the other Canadians?" Franklin asked.

"I am coming to that," Richardson went on. "I say that we *believed* his story, but afterwards we became convinced from circumstances that it had not been wolf meat at all."

"What was it?"

Richardson lowered his eyes. "You asked about the Canadians . . ."

Franklin's eyes opened wide in disbelief. "You mean—" His mouth became dry.

"Yes. It must have been human flesh. The question is whether he actually murdered the Canadians or found their bodies in the snow."

"We cannot prove it, of course," said Franklin. "I suggest that Michel destroyed one of them, then had to kill the others to avoid detection. Then he—well, a hungry man may do anything. What happened then?"

"Michel became highly irritable. We avoided as much as possible conversing upon the hopelessness of our situation. Rather we tried to talk about the happy prospects of our future. The fact is that with the decay of our strength, our minds decayed, and we were no longer able to bear the contemplation of the horrors that surrounded us."

"That does not excuse Michel."

"Not at all, but it does explain his behavior. It got to the point where he refused to hunt, or to help carry wood. He argued with Hood. Finally one day he made a remarkable statement. He said: 'It is no use hunting. There are no animals. You had better kill and eat me.'

"On the twentieth of October, both Hepburn and I were away from the tent when we heard a shot. I returned to find poor Hood lying lifeless at the fireside, a ball having apparently entered his forehead. At first I thought he had done it himself. On examining the body, I discovered that the shot had entered the back of the head, and passed out at the forehead. The gun, fired from close range, was of the longest kind supplied to the Indians. It therefore could not have been placed in a position to inflict such a wound except by a second person."

"You asked Michel how it happened?"

"He said it was an accident. But from that moment on, Michel knew that we knew. He became more hostile. When we broke up camp and resumed our march, he watched our every move. He muttered to himself. He told us he wouldn't come with us, that southward was the better way. I told him if that was the way he felt, he could go south. This only made him more angry and dangerous.

"I cannot describe to you every event that occurred. He threatened Hepburn. He said he hated all white people. In short, I came to the conclusion that he had gone completely mad and would attempt to destroy us as soon as he could. Since Hepburn and I together could not resist him if he attacked—armed as he was with gun, bayonet, pistols, and a knife—I knew that I had to take his life.

"Finally at one point he halted, and was gone a few moments. I knew and Hepburn knew that he had gone to put his gun in order. Both of us no longer doubted that he was about to attack. And so, when he returned, I . . .'"

Richardson trailed off. There was no need to go on. Franklin understood. It was a law of the Arctic, a law of men, a law of self defense.

In their lonely fort in the silent wilderness, there was little the thin and helpless survivors could do but wait—for help or for death. There was nothing more they could do but crawl for firewood and try to swallow some *tripe de roche*.

They grew weaker and weaker. On the evening of November 1, Peltier died and, a few hours later, Semandre died also. So weak were the rest that they could not even bury their comrades, or take them down to the river. They could only drag them to another room, and then collapse from exhaustion.

On the third of November they ate the last of the bones. By now they were able to gather only enough wood at a time for twelve hours' fire. They talked as cheerfully as possible, and read the Bible. All looked like ghosts, with dilated eyes, and spoke in low and guttural voices.

"In proportion as our strength decayed," Franklin wrote, "our minds exhibited symptoms of weakness, evinced by a kind of unreasonable pettishness with each other. Each of us thought the other weaker in intellect than himself, and more in need of advice and assistance. So trifling a circumstance as a change of place, recommended by one as being warmer and more comfortable, and refused by the other from a dread of motion, frequently called forth fretful expressions which were no sooner uttered than atoned for, to be repeated perhaps in the course of a few minutes."

On the morning of November 7 they heard the report of a musket. The doctor and Hepburn, out after wood, could hardly believe that anyone was near.

Then came a shout and they saw three Indians close to the house. Richardson went inside as fast as he could.

"The Indians, sir. The Indians have arrived!"

Tears came to their eyes. Franklin bowed his head immediately and said: "Praise be to the Almighty for our deliverance."

Back, they learned, had staggered, almost dead, to the Indians' tents and told them what had happened. Now one of the Indians approached the starving men and opened a deerskin bag. In it were dried deer meat, some fat, and a few old tongues.

To Franklin, Richardson, and Hepburn it was—at that moment—the most wonderful sight on earth.

Seventeen

ENGLAND

Franklin and his companions spent the winter of 1821–22 in northern Canada and, during the following summer, trekked back to York Factory and sailed for home. When they arrived in England in October, 1822, it was to a hero's welcome.

As soon as he wrote and published his *Narrative of a Journey to the Shores of the Polar Sea*, Franklin's name became almost a household word. It was certainly a name to be reckoned with in society, and Franklin found himself in a whirl of dinners, balls, and meetings.

He was elected to the Royal Society—an honor transcending most others—and promoted to the rank of captain. No one doubted that he deserved every honor, for all the hardships he had endured for England.

But Captain Franklin, though he enjoyed these accolades, did not remain content. He was restless. His life, his hopes, his ambitions lay across the sea, in the cold and lonely lands of the Arctic. The Northwest Passage was out there somewhere. It had to be found, and he was more determined than ever to find it. Accordingly, he began to plan another expedition.

Meanwhile, there was something else to be attended to. The Arctic was not John Franklin's only love. He had another, and it was a different kind.

Captain John Franklin, after his return from the first journey to the shores of the Polar Seas. He was probably about thirty-six years old. (Engraved by W. T. Fry from a drawing by T. Wageman)

She was young, gentle, and beautiful. She had a round face with large, dark eyes, and from her bearing one could tell at once that she was a woman of considerable intelligence. Eleanor Anne Porden, daughter of an eminent architect, had met Franklin before he went to Canada. How much he was impressed with her can be guessed by the fact that he had given the name Porden Islands to a group of islets in the Polar Sea.

Now he and Eleanor were together again. Who can tell what was in their hearts as the birch leaves opened and the finches sang in that spring of 1823? What would

a captain and his lady say to each other as they strolled
beside the coppices bespangled with primroses and blue-
bells? Or walked along the cliffs at the edge of the sea,
with the wind swirling her calico dress and fluttering the
ribbons on her straw bonnet? He might have stopped and
looked at her and said:

"There is an old saying, my dear Eleanor, that she
who weds a sailor weds also the sea."

"Yes? And do you think I am unaware of it?"

"That, above all, must be clear. Whatever comes, whatever happens, I . . ."

She probably nodded and lowered her eyes, as if she
had always understood.

"You are going back to Canada."

". . . I must accept any service, however perilous. Yes
—I am going back. The Duke of Clarence has approved
my plan for finishing the survey."

"After what you have been through?"

"My job in Canada has only begun. I shall not rest a
day until I examine the coast west of the Coppermine
River . . . until I find the Northwest Passage."

"Your heart is set on it. I know that. I know also what
I must do, and that is to help you. But promise me one
thing—If I make a flag, will you carry it? Will you fly it
on the shore of the Polar Sea?"

He would have looked at her for a moment, puzzled,
and then said: "I promise."

They were married on August 19, 1823, and the following summer Eleanor Franklin gave birth to a daughter,
who was named Eleanor after her mother. These were
happy times, but soon to be saddened, for it became ap-

Eleanor Anne Porden Franklin

parent that the mother had a chest disease that was growing serious.

Meanwhile, John Franklin busily made arrangements for his coming expedition. This time he vowed that he would be fully prepared. With a disastrous experience behind to serve as a guide, he took every precaution to prevent the same thing from happening again.

He arranged for the Hudson's Bay Company to convey his entire provisions and party to Great Bear Lake. He intended to float down the Mackenzie River to its mouth and from there send parties east and west to explore the shores of the Polar Sea. No more would he have to use frail canoes; he ordered boats constructed that would be strong enough to withstand waves at sea. No more would he have to do without food or clothing or ammunition.

Perhaps this time he would find the Eskimos, too. Perhaps he would meet Parry. Back in 1819, while Franklin had sailed to Hudson Bay, Parry had sailed into Baffin Bay and entered Lancaster Sound. Going west, without much ice to impede their progress, Parry's ships became the first to sail into Barrow Strait, Prince Regent Inlet, and Wellington Channel.

Parry and his party wintered on the south coast of Melville Island, farther west than any had sailed—above the Arctic Circle. In the summer of 1820 his route to the west was blocked with ice, and so he returned to England; yet from what he had seen he was convinced that the Northwest Passage existed, and that he had been on the verge of discovering it.

The following year, while members of Franklin's party in two canoes were exploring the coast of Canada and then returning nearly starved to Fort Enterprise, Parry had led another pair of ships into Arctic seas. This time, however, he sailed through Hudson Strait into Repulse Bay and got as far as Fury and Hecla Strait, but ice prevented his going farther. By the time he returned, John Franklin had also returned, and by 1825 the grandest plan of all was taking shape—a three-pronged attack on the problem of finding the Northwest Passage.

Approaching from the east would be Parry, who was now convinced that the route lay by way of Lancaster Sound, and thence either through Prince Regent Inlet to the south or Barrow Strait to the west.

Approaching from the west would be Captain Beechey, in H.M.S. *Blossom,* sailing around Alaska to Kotzebue Inlet in Bering Strait.

Approaching from the south, by land, would be Franklin (with Richardson and Back again his officers), down the Mackenzie River and finally sailing along the northern coasts. If he got far enough to the west, he would contact Beechey. If he got far enough to the east, he would contact Parry. What a glorious reunion they would have! Such meetings would link forever the lands of Europe to the lands of the Orient through the legendary "passage to Cathay." They would have succeeded in one of the greatest geographical searches in the history of mankind.

As the time drew near for Franklin to depart, he became more worried about his wife. In a letter to his brother-in-law he wrote:

"Hannah's last letter to Mr. Booth will have apprised you of my dearest Eleanor being in a very alarming state. The disease has continued its rapid progress, and she is now to all appearance nearly at her last extremity . . .

"She has desired me to pray for her in express words during the night, and about three hours since asked me to read the chapter of *Corinthians* used for the funeral service . . . She expressed before the whole party her decided wish that I should not delay in going on the expedition, that it has ever been her desire, and that she is not of the opinion that the circumstance of my going has hastened the crisis of her complaint, which she now thinks has been long in progress."

As he sat in anguish by her bed, she said to him: "The doctors say I am rallying; did they tell you that?"

"Yes," he replied. "They say you have taken a turn for the better."

She handed him a small paper box. "Here is a present for you."

British flag on the beach near Mount Conybeare. This engraving, from an original drawing by Back, may represent the flag made by Mrs. Franklin

He opened it and pulled out a hand-sewn British flag of pure silk.

"I made it as I promised, you see," she said. "Now you must promise me one thing about it."

"What is it, my dearest?"

"That you will not display this flag until you have reached the Polar Sea."

He looked at her and smiled again, as he had done that day at the edge of the sea. "I promise," he said.

Eighteen

MACKENZIE RIVER

The officers of the expedition sailed in an American packet ship and arrived in New York in March, 1825. During the short time they were in New York City, Franklin one evening attended a theatre and afterwards wrote his impressions of it.

"It is a neat house and happened to be well filled," he said. "Some of the gentlemen, however, sat with their hats on in the boxes by the side of the ladies. So much for a young country, and for liberty and independence!"

He did not remain long. The route to Canada led past Albany and Niagara Falls. As he traveled in the young and struggling United States, he was impressed by "the industry of the American character evinced by the number of the towns and villages which have sprung up within a few years, and where there was every appearance of prosperity and comfort . . . I certainly have no partiality either for the Americans or for their Constitution, but it is impossible not to admire their industry." So he wrote in a letter to his wife.

But Eleanor Franklin did not receive the letter. News arrived informing the captain that his wife had died just two months before—scarcely seven days after he had sailed from England. On hearing this, his senses were blunted with grief and sadness. He wrote his sister:

"I have just received through the newspaper, "an account of the death of my dearest Eleanor. You can imagine my distress, as I had hoped from the change which had taken place two days before my departure that her life might have been spared . . . I feel deeply for my dearest child, though I know she will receive from Isabella [Franklin's sister] a mother's anxious love, yet to a tender female a mother's loss is irreparable. I earnestly pray God to protect her, and that she may be brought up in His love."

He must have packed his gear that morninig with a heavy heart. Yet there was no choice: he could neither halt nor turn back.

In two canoes, the party sailed across Lakes Huron and Superior to Fort William, thence to Cumberland House, back on the Saskatchewan River that was so familiar to them. For most of the way through Canada they followed the same route as before, northward to Fort Chipewyan and then to Fort Resolution (see map, page 185). At Great Slave Lake they turned westward into new territory, and started down the Mackenzie River on their long and winding course northwest to the Polar Sea.

They arrived at Fort Norman on August 7, having made good time. Here the party separated. Dr. Richardson headed east to explore the northern shore of Great Bear Lake. Back took charge of the construction of winter quarters for the entire expedition.

Franklin and nine others, in one of the boats, continued down the Mackenzie to scout out ice conditions at the edge of the sea. They wanted to study the prospects of advancing along the coast next summer, and to ascertain the trend of the coast in both directions from the mouth of the river. They would also see whether any provisions could be secured along the coasts.

So broad was the Mackenzie River—over two miles

wide in places—and so swift the current, that the little boat floated rapidly downstream. In two days they reached Fort Good Hope, most northern of the Hudson's Bay Company posts. In three days more they reached the northern ocean.

To their great delight, it was entirely devoid of ice. Seals and whales swam through the waters. In all directions, conditions for navigation appeared to be entirely favorable. Wait until next summer, Franklin thought. An open sea like this must mean a Northwest Passage that was free of ice. He felt a twinge of impatience mingled with hope. Next June they would have three months to explore to the east and west of here, to meet Captain Beechey's ships as they approached from Alaska, and Parry's as they came from the east.

While he stood there, gazing spiritedly out across the Polar Sea, Franklin's thoughts sailed far away. He thought of England, and of the death of his wife. He remembered her flag, and the promise he had made. Drawing the flag from the small case, he mounted it on a pole and raised it at the edge of the sea. He stepped back and stood for a long while, looking first at the flag, then at the sea, and then far away into time and distance. He bowed his head.

In the cool salt breeze sweeping in to the shore, the silk flag curled and folded gently, quietly, brilliantly in the Arctic sun. John Franklin stood beside it for a long, long time.

By the fifth of September, 1825, all members of the expedition returned to the winter quarters which Back had built on Great Bear Lake and named Fort Franklin in honor of his commander.

Winter view of Fort Franklin. (Engraved from a drawing by George Back, under whose command the outpost was constructed)

"We are snugly seated in our winter quarters," Franklin wrote in a letter one November day. "They form three sides of a square, the centre house being occupied by the officer, the buildings on its left by the men, and on its right is a store . . .

"Our house contains a spacious hall, and on each side of it are two apartments which are fitted up according to the taste and means of the occupiers. Dr. Richardson and myself are in one of these, which is neatly whitewashed and ornamented with books, instruments, clothes, and beds . . . My limbs repose nightly on a well-stuffed bed, covered with leather, between good, warm blankets, and, as you may suppose, I sleep soundly.

"The season of darkness is daily advancing, and in the height of winter we must not expect to have more than five hours' light, so that we may have sleep to our hearts' content. We generally, however, sit up till midnight, reading or employed otherwise, and rise about eight o'clock, have our breakfast directly, dinner at half-past five, and tea at nine.

"The evening is passed away often in a game at chess or some sport, and the day devoted to business. We are about to establish a school for the instruction of the men; and on Sundays Divine Service with sermons is held twice, and it is a real gratification to find the men joining on these occasions with great fervency and attention."

Late in May spring came, and the Fort bustled with activity as the separate parties readied for their departure. Franklin's two boats, named *Lion* and *Reliance,* resembled each other, being six feet wide and twenty-six long, and made of fir with birch cross-timbers.

The men were issued sky-blue waterproof uniforms and warm outer clothing. Into the boats went blankets, tools, medicine, food, and presents for the Eskimos— whom they now felt certain they would meet. When the loading was finished, Franklin explained to the entire party the purposes of the voyages and then, as he wrote it in his journal: "This interesting day was closed by the consumption of a small quantity of rum, reserved for the occasion, followed by a merry dance, in which all joined with great glee . . ."

Finally they were off. Franklin, accompanied by Lieutenant Back, the interpreter, Augustus, and thirteen other men, shoved off in the *Lion* and *Reliance*. Richardson and his party followed in their boats. Going downriver, they made good time, despite the streams of ice that sailed past. Once they stopped at a place where Alexander

Mackenzie in 1789 had seen flames rising from a bank. It was a vein of coal on fire and now, thirty-seven years later, smoke still issued from several fissures in the ground. Wild onions grew along the banks of the river.

Melting ice had rendered the banks so soft that, when the men walked along the river's edge, they would sink to their knees in mud.

Yet no hardship was as difficult to endure as the mosquitoes, which now swarmed everywhere. Sometimes when the boats landed in the evening for dinner, the mosquitoes beset the weary travelers so furiously that they were forced to reembark and sail on. Even that did not help, for the mosquitoes pursued them out on the river and deprived them of rest.

At Fort Good Hope they learned that a party of Eskimos had been seen downriver. "Where were they going?" Franklin asked. "What are their movements?"

No one answered. No one knew. But the rumors encouraged Franklin. He knew that he was getting close. After leaving Fort Good Hope they entered Eskimo territory and stopped one morning to clean their weapons, and to issue a gun, a dagger, and ammunition to every man.

On the third of July, as they neared the Mackenzie River delta, where the river divided into many channels, the two parties separated. Dr. Richardson and his boats turned eastward to explore the coast of Canada north and east of the Mackenzie River, hoping to get as far as the Coppermine River.

With the hearty farewell cheers of Richardson's group in their ears, Franklin's party set off along a westerly channel of the Mackenzie. Floating along on the peaceful current he remembered how different things were on their disastrous voyage five years before. Instead of frail canoes

Chronometer used by John Franklin on his second expedition through Canada to the Polar Sea (1825-1827)

and a scant supply of food, they now had excellent boats, with a three-months' store of provisions.

They pulled ashore at the mouth of the river and Franklin stepped out to take an observation for latitude, as well as to make some notes. Hardly had he walked around a headland and along the beach when he spied an island on the eastern side of the bay. It was like most other Arctic islands, except that this one held what he had long been waiting to see.

The island was crowded with Indian tents and, strolling among them, were the owners themselves. He had discovered the Eskimos at last.

Nineteen

THE ESKIMOS

Franklin hurried back to the boats. Guns were inspected, stores covered with canvas, and presents made ready.

"I wish to make it clear," Franklin told them, "that there must be no bloodshed. In the past, much sacrifice of life has resulted from people mistaking noise and violent gestures for signs of attack. Your orders are not to fire until I set the example, or until you are ordered to do so by Lieutenant Back."

Boarding the boats, they pushed away from shore and steered toward the island under easy sail, ensigns flying. Franklin described the encounter in his journal, calling the Indians "Esquimaux"—a French spelling that was common in his day.

"The water became shallow as we drew towards the island, and the boats touched the ground when about a mile from the beach; we shouted, and made signs to the Esquimaux to come off, and then pulled a short way back to await their arrival . . .

"Three canoes instantly put off from shore, and before they could reach us others were launched in such quick succession, that the whole space between the island and the boats was covered by them.

"The Esquimaux canoes contain only one person, and are named *kaiyacks;* but they have a kind of open boat capable of holding six or eight people, which is named *oomiak*. The men alone use the kaiyacks, and the oomiaks are allotted to the women and children.

"We endeavored to count their numbers as they approached, and had proceeded as far as seventy-three canoes and five oomiaks, when the sea became so crowded by fresh arrivals, that we could advance no farther in our reckoning."

Augustus, the interpreter, hailed them as soon as they came within speaking range. "We come as friends," he shouted. "We have presents for you. Please come and accept our gifts, O chiefs."

The Eskimo chiefs, in the first three boats, seemed reluctant to approach. Augustus then explained that this expedition was hunting a passage through the Polar Sea. "If we discover such a passage," he said in Eskimo, "big ships will bring good things for you and your people."

The chiefs repeated these remarks to their followers, whereupon, as Franklin describes it, "they testified their joy by tossing their hands aloft, and raising the most deafening shout of applause I ever heard."

The chiefs approached and took the presents offered. They then gave Franklin the knives and ornaments worn on their heads and arms. Franklin studied them closely. They were different from other natives of the northern territories because their cheekbones did not protrude so far. The small eyes and broad nose were characteristic. The faces were tattooed. Hair grew on the upper lip and chin, and the hair on the head was long and straight. Every man had pieces of bone or shell thrust through the septum of his nose. In holes in the lower lip were circular pieces of ivory with a blue bead in the center.

The Eskimo dress consisted of jackets, skirts, and

hoods of caribou skin, and boots cut out of seal skin. They carried bows and arrows and all were armed with knives.

"Up to this time the first three were the only kaiyacks that had ventured near the boats," wrote Franklin, "but the natives around us had now increased to two hundred and fifty or three hundred persons, and they . . . pressed eagerly upon us, offering for sale their bows, arrows, and spears, which they had hitherto kept concealed within their canoes."

Try as he might, in the general din Franklin could not get information about the coast. He therefore ordered that the boat be turned around and the parties readied to leave. When this was translated by Augustus, the Eskimos turned to and helped push the canoes around in the shallow water.

At that moment, an oar from the *Lion* struck one of the Eskimo kayaks, upset it, and plunged its owner head foremost into the water and mud.

"We instantly extricated him from his unpleasant situation," wrote Franklin, "and took him into the boat until the water could be thrown out of his *kaiyak*, and Augustus, seeing him shivering with cold, wrapped him up in his own great coat.

"At first he was exceedingly angry, but soon became reconciled to his situation, and looking aboard, discovered that we had many . . . articles in the boat . . . He soon began to ask for everything he saw, and expressed much displeasure on our refusing to comply with his demands."

As soon as the Eskimo shouted to all the others that riches lay in the white men's canoes, the rush was on. Franklin and his men resisted as well as they could, but the Eskimos were determined to climb into the canoes.

The chiefs then said that if they were allowed to come in, the others would stay out. Franklin assented. At that moment, one of the Englishmen saw that the Eskimo whose kayak had been upset carried under his belt a pistol stolen from Lieutenant Back. Realizing that he had been discovered, the Eskimo leaped out of the boat—still wearing the coat that Augustus had wrapped around him.

The situation turned into utter confusion. The *Lion* had by now become stuck in the mud because of an ebbing tide. Franklin ordered Augustus to tell the Indians that if they would stay back, he would go to meet the ship that they were expecting and later return with a greater supply of presents. This seemed to satisfy the Eskimos. They stepped back—but not for long. Soon they were pushing and pulling again, and this time succeeded in getting the English boats ashore.

"Two of the most powerful men, jumping on board at the same time," Franklin wrote, "seized me by the wrists and forced me to sit between them; and as I shook them loose two or three times, a third Esquimaux took his station in front to catch my arm whenever I attempted to lift my gun, or the broad dagger which hung by my side . . .

"A numerous party then . . . began a regular pillage, handing the articles to the women, who, ranged in a row behind, quickly conveyed them out of sight. Lieutenant Back and his crew strenuously, but good-humoredly resisted the attack, and rescued many things from their grasp, but they were overpowered by numbers, and had even some difficulty in preserving their arms.

"One fellow had the audacity to snatch Vivier's knife from his breast, and to cut the buttons from his coat, whilst three stout Esquimaux surrounded Lieutenant Back with uplifted daggers, and were incessant in their demands for whatever attracted their attention, especially for the anchor buttons which he wore on his waistcoat."

Above: Franklin and his party, in the *Lion* and *Reliance,* being approached, about a mile from the mouth of the Mackenzie River, by Eskimos in kayaks and oomiaks. *Below:* Eskimos pillaging Franklin's boats. (Both pictures were engraved from drawings by George Back)

Meanwhile, the Eskimos had begun in earnest to plunder the *Lion*. The sides of the boat were "lined with men as thick as they could stand, brandishing their knives in the most furious manner, and attempting to seize everything that was movable."

So outnumbered were Franklin's men that they could not prevent some things from being carried entirely away. It was all they could do to protect the guns, the oars, the masts that they needed for defense and transportation.

"In the whole of this unequal contest," Franklin continued, "the self-possession of our men was not more conspicuous than the coolness with which the Esquimaux received the heavy blows dealt to them with the butts of the muskets. But at length, irritated at being so often foiled in their attempts, several of them jumped on board and forcibly endeavored to take the daggers and shot-belts that were about the men's persons; and I myself engaged with three of them who were trying to disarm me . . .

"I then saw that my crew were nearly overpowered in the fore part of the boat, and hastening to their aid, I fortunately arrived in time to prevent George Wilson from discharging the contents of his musket into the body of an Esquimaux. He had received a provocation of which I was ignorant until the next day, for the fellow had struck at him with a knife, and cut through his coat and waistcoat; and it was only after the affray was over that I learned that Gustavus Aird, the bowman of the *Lion,* and three of the *Reliance's* crew, had also narrowly escaped from being wounded, their clothes being cut by the blows made at them with knives.

"No sooner was the bow cleared of one set of marauders than another party commenced their operations at the stern. My gun was now the object of the struggle, which was beginning to assume a more serious complexion, when the whole of the Esquimaux suddenly fled, and hid themselves behind the drift timber on the beach."

Looking around, Franklin saw why. Back's men stood with muskets leveled. Seeing this, the Eskimos had fled in panic.

"Let's get out of here," Franklin shouted.

No sooner had the canoes floated and moved away from shore, than the Eskimos leaped into their canoes and started to follow.

"Augustus!" Franklin called.

"Yes, sir?" replied the interpreter.

"Tell them that I shall shoot the first man to come within range of our muskets."

Augustus translated. The Eskimos stopped. The *Lion* and *Reliance* moved swiftly across the bay and soon left the village far behind.

They named the place Pillage Point. As he thought over the adventure of that day, Franklin must have given a sigh of relief.

"I cannot sufficiently praise the fortitude and obedience of both the boats' crews," he wrote, "in abstaining from the use of their arms. In the first instance I had been influenced by the desire of preventing unnecessary bloodshed, and afterwards, when the critical situation of my party might have well warranted me in employing more decided means for their defence, I still endeavored to temporize, being convinced that as long as the boats lay aground, and we were beset by such numbers, armed with long knives, bows, arrows, and spears, we could not use fire-arms to advantage.

"The howling of the women, and the clamor of the men, proved the high excitement to which they had wrought themselves; and I am still of opinion that, mingled as we were with them, the first blood we had shed would have been instantly revenged by the sacrifice of all our lives."

The wind became fair, and the two boats set sail for

the northwest, along the coast of the Polar Sea. Soon, however, they were blocked by ice that had not yet broken from shore. They learned from some Eskimos they met that farther west the ice was often frozen to the land throughout the summer.

And so the little party now began the vexing task of working slowly along the coast, of setting out to sea when they found an open channel, and of running quickly into shore when the ice closed in dangerously. Sometimes in high winds they had to stay in camp for days. Sometimes the mosquitoes tormented them so severely that the only escape was to remain in their smoke-filled tents. Or if wind and frozen sea did not delay them, there was fog, thick fog that blotted out the ice, the sea, and the shore.

Even so, they did the best they could. When the fog lifted, Back sketched the scenery along the coast and carefully drew his maps and charts. Franklin collected rocks and minerals, and preserved between sheets of paper some of the flowers that grew along the coast. From time to time they saw whales swimming among the icebergs out to sea.

Franklin also made observations on longitude, and on the magnetic variations of the compass. There was no end to the astronomical observations to be made. By lunar readings they confirmed the rates of the timekeepers. They kept careful watch to be sure that the chronometers functioned accurately. From these instruments and readings they recorded their progress westward through the degrees of longitude . . . 136° . . . 137° . . . 138° . . .

Ice or no ice, they kept on moving west. Walking was difficult, especially under their heavy burdens, because most of the coast was swampy. Whenever they came to an open channel in the ice, however, they would load and launch the boats. Sometimes they had to break through ice with hatchets and poles to reach clear water. But then the wind would rise, the ice would close in, and they would flee to land. This happened again and again, exhausting their patience.

Whenever he could, Augustus visited Eskimo encampments along the way. At Herschel Island they visited Eskimos and saw a large herd of caribou. Farther on, through swamps and mosquitoes, they hiked to the top of Mount Conybeare and from there had a commanding view of the wilderness mountains to the south.

They passed 141° West Longitude, the boundary between British and Russian territory. They kept a constant lookout for Beechey's ship, the *Blossom*. It could be that

Traveling among the icebergs off the Arctic coasts of Canada and Alaska, Franklin and his companions saw majestic scenes like this. (Engraved from original drawing of George Back)

Beechey would send small boats to try to contact them, or perhaps would try to reach Franklin's party by means of an overland journey. Beechey must surely be off Icy Cape by now. (As a matter of fact, he was, and he did send a boat east along the Russian coast. Though no one knew it at the time, this boat of Beechey's reached within 160 miles of Franklin's westernmost advance. Had the weather been better, or the sea more open, the two expeditions might easily have made a historic contact.)

The *Lion* and *Reliance* moved on, and when Franklin arrived at a place named by him Cape Beechey—149° West Longitude—he knew that he could go no farther. The thickness of the ice had delayed them. The sun began to set each day before midnight—a stern reminder that summer was waning. Gales had already become fierce enough to blow down the expedition's tents.

If they were to go back to the Mackenzie River at all, Franklin knew, they had to start early. So on the 16th of August, 1826, they turned and retraced their route to the Mackenzie River and up this to Fort Franklin, reaching there five weeks later. They had traveled 2,048 miles, of which 374 were previously unknown coastline of Canada and Alaska.

Dr. Richardson and his party, meanwhile, had navigated the coast from the mouth of the Mackenzie to the mouth of the Coppermine River—discovering 863 miles of Canadian shore.

Franklin spent the winter at Fort Franklin, and Richardson at Cumberland House. In 1827 they returned to England, proud of what they had accomplished, but knowing fully that unless Parry had succeeded in his attempt, the Northwest Passage had not yet been conquered.

141° W

100° W

"POLAR SEA"

T OF FRANKLIN'S
OGRESS 1826

Beechey Point
Cape Beechey)

ANKLIN
NTAINS
Mt. Conybeare

HERSCHEL
ISLAND

RICHARDSON'S ROUTE

RICHARDSON
MOUNTAINS

Great Bear
Lake

Coppermine
River

ARCTIC CIRCLE

Fort
Good Hope

Mackenzie

Fort
Franklin

Fort Norman

FRANKLIN'S River

ROUTE

Great Slave
Lake

Fort
Resolution

Slave River

CANADA

COPYRIGHT BY RAND MC NALLY & COMPANY

**Franklin's route (solid line) and Richardson's route
(dashes) as described in Chapters 18 and 19**

Twenty

THE MEDITERRANEAN

As soon as he possibly could, Franklin sought out Parry to exchange information. Parry's expedition, which was supposed to have navigated the Northwest Passage by sea from the east, had met with failure. His ships had been gripped by the ice and one of them was wrecked.

Still, Franklin was convinced that the passage existed, and that it was soon to be discovered. Apparently the Admiralty felt the same way. The Lord High Admiral asked Franklin to prepare a full plan for completion of the survey of the northern coast of America. Franklin did.

It would be necessary, he wrote, to explore the unknown coast east of where he had stopped on his earlier expedition. He proposed a new voyage to do that first.

Second, there must be an overland journey east of Great Slave Lake, where a river, according to the Indians, flowed into the Polar Sea. The explorers could go down that river, map the coast, and join the vessels that came by sea.

And just in case anyone should forget who would like to command one of these expeditions, Franklin closed his plan by saying: "I hope your Royal Highness will permit me to solicit the honour of an appointment to one of them."

There could be no doubt of his ability, for once again

the world acclaimed the heroic Captain Franklin. Based on his new book, *Narrative of a Second Expedition to the Shores of the Polar Sea,* geographers added new details to their maps, and scientists evaluated the information on minerals, rocks, plants, and astronomical phenomena. Everyone else found thrills aplenty in the adventures themselves.

Franklin spent what time he could with his little daughter Eleanor, who now was four, and still under the affectionate care of his sister.

At this time, too, Franklin was on the way toward his second marriage. He had known Jane Griffin even before going on his second Canadian expedition—and indeed had named in her honor a point of land on the Alaskan coast. Jane Griffin had been a friend of Eleanor Franklin. She was the daughter of a well-to-do lawyer—a beautiful and good-humored woman, and a dignified one. She had dark hair and large, dark eyes that could flash with excitement.

Don't be alarmed, she wrote him, if she changed rapidly—sometimes serious, sometimes gay. That was her way. She also knew her duty to love, yet even so, she said, "my ring will not be a badge of slavery, but the cherished link of the purest affection."

Word arrived from the Admiralty regarding Franklin's plan for further Arctic expeditions, and the word was bad. No new expeditions would be recommended to His Majesty's Government.

For once, Franklin was so busy that he didn't have time to think very much about his disappointment, and if he had, he would probably have concluded that the Admiralty would soon change its mind anyway. Discovery

Sir John Franklin, from a portrait made about the time he was knighted in 1829. He was then 43

of the Northwest Passage was still as urgent a matter as always, something the nation would accomplish in time—unless some other country found it first.

Until then, Franklin had work to do. He went on an official tour of Russia, where he dined at a party given by the Empress herself. On returning to England he went to Hughington to see his old commander of the *Bellerophon*, Captain Cumby. The date was October 21, 1828, an anniversary of the memorable Battle of Trafalgar, which date it was the captain's practice to celebrate each year.

"On the church steeple," Franklin wrote in a letter to Jane, "the flag under which the old *Bellerophon* fought was waving, with many of its shot-holes still unclosed, and you can well conceive the delight it afforded to me, especially as the preservation of it in the hour of battle was one of the particular parts of my duty as signal officer."

As he watched, his mind went back to the tremendous excitement of that day, more than two decades ago.

John Franklin and Jane Griffin were married on the fifth of November, 1828, and soon after were in Paris, engulfed in high society. Franklin dined with the eminent scientist, Baron Cuvier, and the banker, Baron Rothschild. He also dined with the Duke of Orleans, who, two years later, was to become the King of France.

For Franklin, the honors continued. The Paris Geographical Society awarded him its gold medal for distinguished service in exploration. He stood beside Captain Parry in Oxford University, England, to receive the honorary degree of D.C.L.—Doctor of Civil Law.

Then on April 29, 1829, he received his highest honor —he was elevated to the Knighthood. Henceforth he would be known to the world as Sir John Franklin.

In 1830, he was appointed to command the 26-gun frigate *Rainbow* and, for the next three years, patrolled the troubled waters of the Mediterranean Sea—especially in the vicinity of Greece. This nation had just won its independence and was going through difficult times.

As senior British naval officer in Greece, Sir John was to land his men for the preservation of law and order and for protection of the Greeks from rebel soldiers. So well did he preserve the peace that King Otho conferred upon him the honor of Knight of the Redeemer of Greece.

Portrait of Lady Jane Franklin, attributed to Thomas Bock

During all this time—while Franklin was stationed at Malta, or Corfu, or off Patras, where most of the trouble occurred, or on patrol in the Gulf of Corinth—he saw very little of Lady Franklin. She was traveling also—to Egypt, the Holy Land, and Greece. These travels were pleasant enough, but Sir John and his lady were too often apart to suit either of them.

By the end of 1833, Franklin was once again in England, and once again "out of work." He had an audience with King William and dined with the king and queen, a thrilling milestone in any Englishman's career.

But he was still restless. When Lady Franklin returned from her travels, they took up residence in London, and from then on Franklin continued to apply for a position of responsibility and dignity with the Navy, or with some other branch of government. Mostly, of course, he wanted to get back to the Arctic. But even though the Northwest Passage and the North Pole still lay undiscovered, public interest in the Arctic—for the moment at least—had waned.

A private expedition led by Sir John Ross, who was accompanied by his nephew James Ross, went out in 1829. They discovered the north magnetic pole, a point on the earth's surface which slowly moves with the changing magnetism of the earth, and was at that time about 1,300 miles from the geographic North Pole. Their ship, however, was frozen so solidly in ice that they had to abandon it. After four winters in the Arctic they were finally rescued by a whaler.

Franklin hoped in vain to conduct an expedition of his own. Once he wrote in a letter:

"You ask . . . what my prospects are. At present I have no employment in view, though I have made application for it in common with many others. Having been recently afloat, and there being but few ships in commission, I cannot expect to be preferred before many other officers of merit. I keep, however, on the watch for anything that may offer."

His old friend Lieutenant Back, now Sir George Back, finished a successful exploration trip in Canada, tracing the Great Fish River to its mouth, and getting as far north as King William Island.

That was about all. The British public and the government seemed to have abandoned interest in the North.

In 1836, the Colonial Secretary, Lord Glenelg, offered Franklin the position of Governor of Antigua, a small island in the British West Indies. Sir John felt that his experience and place in life equipped him for a higher position than that. He declined.

Then, scarcely two weeks afterward, he was asked to take the post of Governor of Van Diemen's Land—the island of Tasmania off the southern tip of Australia.

Now that was more like it! Once again all the thrills and adventures of his voyage with Flinders—thirty-five years before—came to him. In his mind's eye he could clearly see the jutting headlands, the forests of eucalyptus, the kangaroos leaping across the glades . . . Of course, he replied, he would accept this position at once.

As soon as his appointment was announced, letters of congratulation arrived from his friends everywhere. "It is to me a matter of most sincere rejoicing," said one, "that a growing settlement like Van Diemen's Land will have the benefit of your management and character."

A thousand things had to be done . . . letters to answer, people to see, things to buy, farewell dinners . . . Despite the many friends who called at their home, Sir John, his daughter Eleanor, and Lady Franklin managed to oversee the packing of their belongings. They sailed in the autumn of 1836. As they departed, one can well imagine the conversation on the streets of London:

"That poor dear man! Whatever are they thinking of to appoint him to such a place?"

"What do you mean?"

"Don't you know? Van Diemen's Land is a convict colony! It is the prison of the Empire. Hardened criminals go there, the worst of rascals. Why, Sir John and Lady Franklin won't be safe for a moment . . ."

Twenty-one

TASMANIA

"Where are the prisoners?"

So might one of Franklin's party have asked on arriving in Hobart, the capital of Tasmania. "Where are the prisoners? I've been here three days and haven't seen any."

"Oh, yes you have. The prisoners are everywhere. The porter who brought your luggage, the maid who waited on you, the police agent who inspected your papers on entry . . ."

"Great Scott! You don't mean they are running free?"

"Not quite. You might call them prisoners without a prison. After all, where would they go if they escaped? We are a world away from England."

"But aren't there some desperate criminals?"

"Yes, they are kept under control in the prison camps."

"And have you none at all who have escaped?"

"A few. They are 'bush-rangers.' They live by robbery and violence if they have to. We don't worry about them."

"Then we will have to keep our things locked up and our houses shuttered."

The Tasmanian laughed.

"Not at all! Our homes stand all day with open doors. We never bar our doors or windows at night, either. Life is peaceful here, you will see."

Tasmania was discovered in 1642 by Abel Janszoon Tasman, but he did not name it that. He named it Van Diemen's Land, after the then governor general of the Dutch East Indies. When Sir John Franklin arrived as its second governor in 1837, he found that the colonists did not like their land to be called Van Diemen's Land. They thought of themselves as Tasmanians and their island as Tasmania. They were proud of that name, and of their colony.

It was not an old colony. In fact, the first settlement had taken place about the time Franklin and his shipmates on the *Porpoise* had been stranded on Wreck Reef, 1,500 miles to the north, in 1803.

Tasmania is a mountainous island, its central part being a plateau over 2,000 feet high. Its highest peak, Mount Ossa, rises 5,305 feet. While most of Australia is dry, parts of Tasmania have so much rain that jungle-like growths occur. In former times the island was extensively covered with gum trees and wattles in the dry places, and beech trees in the wet. There are also grass-trees, pines, blackwoods, and tree ferns. Elsewhere stretch button-grass plains and moorlands.

For the most part, Tasmania is a cool land, exposed to westerly and southerly winds. In many ways the Franklins found it similar to England—cool and moist, with little gardens here and there beside the homes, and with blooming bushes of geraniums.

Long before the island had been found by Europeans, a race of natives lived there, perhaps as many as three thousand. By the time of Franklin's arrival this number had been reduced to fewer than fifty, and he knew that some day the entire race would become extinct. This fate, he said, would be a "source of hopeless sorrow."

Launceston, second largest city in Tasmania, as it looks today

Then there were the prisoners. At the time of Franklin's arrival in 1837 nearly 18,000 convicts lived in Tasmania—prisoners sent from all parts of the British Empire for detention there. This gave the island its reputation as a "convict colony." The rest of the island was inhabited by approximately 24,000 free colonists.

One of Franklin's first duties, he knew, was to get acquainted with the people. This was not difficult, especially because the people already knew of him through his famous exploits. When their ship arrived in Hobart, the new governor was met by the Executive Council, the Commandant of Troops, and other officials, as well as by a wildly cheering throng of Tasmanians eager to meet the renowned explorer—the "man who had eaten his shoes."

Sir John and Lady Franklin toured the island, and were everywhere received with rejoicing. So popular was he that on the ride into Launceston, Sir John was escorted by three hundred horsemen and seventy carriages.

"Fame has anticipated Your Excellency's arrival," said a welcoming official. "The history of your life is before us. The qualities of mind and heart which the various arduous and gallant public services successfully conducted by Your Excellency have developed we consider a sure and certain guarantee of just and impartial administration, and of fair dealing toward all men."

The Franklins visited the convict colonies. They crept along underground galleries in coal mines. They dined on kangaroo soup, and ate wallaby joints, trumpeter fish, and other delicacies of the island.

As he settled down to the complex task of governing a complex island, Franklin surveyed the prospects before him. Even in 1837, Tasmania was a busy island. Its industries included shipyards, breweries, tanneries, and foundries. More than three hundred vessels used the island's ports each year. Convicts worked on the public roads and bridges and buildings, keeping them in good order.

Carriages and people on horseback plied the streets of Hobart between the neat stone houses that were roofed with shingles made from slabs of the peppermint gum tree. Riding, racing, and water sports were favorite forms of diversion for the people. They had a theatre, too, where plays were performed and, of course, a heavy schedule of society balls and supper parties.

Franklin thought highly of the Tasmanians. "The original free population," he said of them, "may be com-

Hobart today, with Mt. Wellington in the background, and the Derwent River harbor in the foreground

pared in point of intelligence, order and good conduct with any community."

These prosperous settlers made a great deal of money, yet had little place to spend it, and their assets grew. Life was easy and labor cheap because they had convicts to help in their homes and at their places of work.

Hobart was the center of government, and the center of Hobart was Government House. Here the Franklins, with their staff of secretaries and advisers and helpers (including Sir John's old friend, John Hepburn, the seaman) came to live. It was described as "a confused, irregular pile of building, added to, from time to time, as the increasing wants and importance of the place required. It is devoid alike of beauty, convenience or comfort, although its site is well adapted for business, and commands some of the most charming prospects both of the port and river . . ."

Hobart was beautifully situated on the banks of the Derwent River, along which were pleasant meadows, farms, and gardens. Beyond rose snowy mountains.

In short, life seemed to be entirely happy and peaceful in Tasmania when John Franklin came in 1837.

But, unfortunately, this was only on the surface.

If there was one thing the colonists wanted, it was to handle their own affairs. Yet England ruled Tasmania as if it were a convict colony and little else. Worse yet, other parts of Australia were being given their freedom while Tasmania fumed and fretted and waited in vain. Many of the islanders were defiant toward the government. Newspapers, which by their very nature feed on public alarm, stirred up discontent.

So it was really a hotbed of unrest to which John Franklin came. As governor, he had of course, to serve two interests—those of Great Britain, and those of the colony. He soon discovered how deeply these interests were in conflict, and many a time he had to determine which of the two to favor in making decisions.

The powers of the governor were set forth in the *Book of Rules and Regulations for the Colonial Service*. Sir John could pardon criminals, appoint and suspend officials, and approve or disapprove the laws passed by the colonial legislature. In many ways, the situation resembled that which prevailed in the American colonies more than sixty years before—and which led there, as well, to clamors for independence.

Among other things, the governor was supposed to

improve the schools. Whatever he did, and whatever happened, he had to send to the Colonial Office in England all records of meetings and important events.

He wished it were that easy! As time went on, the Colonial Office too often sent him orders to do things that he knew ought not be done or could not be done. What then? He stood condemned if he did, and condemned if he didn't. If only London would consult him before they made some of their rules!

"Alas, Sir John," said one of his advisors, "you are just an agent for a distant tyranny."

In spite of it all, John Franklin, now nearly 52 years old, set eagerly to work. Day after day he listened to prisoners pleading for better treatment. He talked with businessmen pursuing their separate causes. He dictated to his assistants an endless stream of dispatches to England. He presided over meetings and Executive and Legislative Council sessions, appointed officials and settled disputes.

The formal duties never seemed to end. With Lady Jane he held official balls and dinners, for which he had to dress in a high, stiff collar and long black coat, and be surrounded by society folk in silks and satins, Prussian velvets, and Kerseymeres. How often he must have wished to be walking again beside a sledge on the trail to Great Bear Lake . . .

No sooner had he begun to make decisions than the newspapers started their attacks. "Lord Glenelg," said one, has "sent out a good worthy man like Sir John Franklin to rule an oppressed, irritated, provoked and consequently discontented people, and tied him down by surrounding him with . . . advisors who are the agents and instruments of his predecessor's evil policy."

This implied that Franklin was carrying on the bad things that the governor before him had carried on. The facts were that Franklin had his own ideas and ways of doing things, but he had to work with officials already there. Sometimes he did not agree with them, and plainly said so. That was to lead to more trouble than he could have imagined.

Lady Franklin helped a great deal, though in those days women were not supposed to dabble in their husbands' affairs. She took a serious interest in his work, and used a goodly part of her private fortune to help the island people.

This led to her being accused of meddling, and that led to the suggestion that the governor depended on her to make his decisions for him. (From all that has ever been found in Franklin's papers and his wife's letters, it seems entirely clear that while he asked her opinions and help in affairs of the colony, it was he who made the final decisions.)

He took his job seriously; too much so, perhaps. Night and day, it was work and work and work. Although that was his usual way of doing things, here at the job of government he was an amateur and he knew it. Always before he had been a sailor, an explorer—not a diplomat. He had not been trained in the niceties of government. Just to do passably well in this new and bewildering task took all the time he could give it. But passably well wasn't good enough. He couldn't write dispatches in language as beautiful as that of the Colonial Office, and this lack of skill disturbed him. He didn't know all the rules of his new profession and therefore dared not make decisions as quickly as he knew he should.

The result was that he became over-anxious. In trying

too hard to avoid mistakes he wasted time and energy on trivial things. Even then he made mistakes, and one of these was simply that he relied too much on those who worked for him. Naturally, he turned often to the Colonial Secretary, second most important official in the Tasmanian government—and the one he should have relied on least, had he but known it.

The man who held this position when Franklin arrived was a one-time soldier named John Montagu, who had fought at the Battle of Waterloo. Montagu had given his complete allegiance to the first governor; and when Franklin did not pursue identical policies, Montagu became enraged. He was, moreover, restless, ambitious, daring, and troublesome. He lacked the honesty that every public official needs. Even his mother had long been worried about his inability to tell the truth. His ambition was to became as important as he possibly could, and the sum of his faults was that he didn't care how he did it.

Time went rapidly by. Victoria became the Queen of the British Empire in 1837 and shortly afterward Prince Albert became her husband. In Canada there were rebellions and discontent—but there was also exploration. George Back attempted to locate the Northwest Passage but had to return from Hudson Bay in a damaged ship, the *Terror,* before he could conclude his search.

To Franklin these events seemed far away. To him the schools of Tasmania—few and poor, with almost nothing provided for education of girls—needed more attention than the things that happened in distant lands. Rich people sent their children to school in England. Some children didn't go to school at all.

How then, thought Franklin, could these people ask

for freedom from England? How, without schools and colleges, could they learn to rule themselves? Sir John and Lady Franklin went to work, and accomplished what was to be their crowning achievement in Tasmania.

Franklin founded the system of public schools, and spared no effort in searching for people to run them and to teach in them. Once the grade schools were under way, boys and girls from all over Tasmania went to them. Then Franklin developed a system of high schools and worked toward the founding of a college. When the public money ran out, he used his own, and Lady Franklin bought and donated land on which the schools were built.

The Franklins took a lively interest in a struggling, scientific group that was to become the Royal Society of Tasmania. They founded a natural history museum, later known as the Lady Franklin Museum because she bought the land and paid for the building herself.

Yet all the time, Colonial Secretary Montagu was secretly working against Sir John. Not only did Montagu generally slow down the routine work of the government, but he also tried to interfere with a project to build a college. His hatred for Franklin deepened. In a letter to a friend he wrote: "It was soon apparent that Sir John had undertaken an office for which his professional education and previous habits of life had in no way prepared him. His inaptitude for Public Business and his inexperience in the affairs and science of government could not be concealed. In fact his own frank admissions satisfied everyone upon these points."

As if unmindful, Franklin devoted strenuous efforts to another of his plans for improving Tasmania: to make a better life for the convicts. Up to now, the lash had been freely used as a means of punishment. Franklin opposed this as he opposed the flogging of men on ships at sea. Here in Van Diemen's Land it seemed as if England wanted only to put the prisoners away and keep them out of sight.

Not Franklin. He was convinced that one of the major responsibilities toward prisoners was to try to turn them into decent, law-abiding citizens. Couldn't bad men become good again? As the years went by he did all he could to help the convicts, and Lady Franklin worked to improve the lot of female prisoners.

It was over a convict that Franklin's first real trouble with Montagu arose. One of the prisoners working outside the prisons was convicted of a crime he had committed in Tasmania and was sentenced to jail. It also happened that the man was an excellent worker and a very good cook. After he was sentenced, but before he went to jail, Montagu hired the criminal to work in his own home as a servant.

As soon as the public learned what Montagu had done, the outcry began. Convicted criminals, they said, did not belong in the luxurious homes of public officials.

Franklin had never tolerated dishonesty, and least of all in public service. He ordered Montagu to send the man to prison.

Montagu was furious. He had been publicly embarrassed—and proven dishonest. Franklin had made a fool of him. He concealed most of his anger, but angry he was, and his bitterness grew. "It is painful beyond description," he wrote his friends, "to act under a Governor who has no firmness of character, and the tool of any rogue who will flatter his wife, for she in fact governs."

Low in spirits, worn out, embattled, nagged as always

by the slight deafness that had resulted from the Battle of Trafalgar, Franklin kept at his tasks. His daily work was so demanding that he couldn't even take a holiday. One day at Government House there were seventy callers. Besides them, the governor and his lady usually had some visitors staying as guests. Fortunately, it was a happy home life. Here, young Eleanor Franklin fell in love, and was married later when she and her husband-to-be returned to England.

But Franklin himself continued to work without respite. Lady Franklin wrote to her sister:

"He takes little exercise, loses in some respects even his appetite, creates imaginary evils, asks me if I can bear it if he is recalled in disgrace, and in fact is more agitated and depressed than I have ever seen him before . . . Sir John's sensitiveness is beyond conception and it is in fact a country where people should have hearts of stone and frames of iron."

On top of everything else, finances were bad. The previous governor had left a scant supply of money in the treasury. England did not send enough. Hard times set in, and the people could not ship away their sheep or cattle, timber, wheat, horses, and other exports. The people came to the government for help, and Franklin and his councils and legislature did all they could.

It was no use. Times grew worse.

The apparent peace and prosperity that Franklin had seen on his arrival in Van Diemen's Land now faded away. He had not obtained for the colony a representative government; London refused to grant that. Handling of the convict colony had not gone as he desired. And now, even the prosperity was going.

In the midst of all the gloom, came one of the brightest

**Sir James Clark Ross, from an oil painting
by Stephen Pearce**

moments of Franklin's stay in Tasmania. In 1840 the celebrated explorer James Clark Ross, one of Franklin's closest friends, arrived on his way to Antarctica to make some astronomical observations. Franklin pitched in with vigor to help build an observatory and prepare equipment with which they could take magnetic readings in

Tasmania. For long hours he talked with Ross and his second in command, Captain Francis Crozier, about their polar explorations, and almost certainly Franklin inquired about new prospects for searching out the Northwest Passage.

Ross and Crozier shortly afterwards left in their ships, the *Erebus* and *Terror,* to do research on the Antarctic continent, and Franklin was the last to see them off.

While they were gone, Ross and Crozier made magnetic observations and fixed the position of the South Magnetic Pole. They explored as much as they could of the continent and its great ice shelves. They discovered two volcanic mountains which they named Mount Erebus and Mount Terror, after their vessels, and far to the south named an island after Franklin.

When they returned to Hobart in 1841 the first boat to meet them bore the Governor of Tasmania himself— eager as always for news of discovery. With the *Erebus* and *Terror* back in Hobart, a season of festivity and gaiety began, with celebrations honoring the two ships and their captains, and even a ball on the *Erebus.* Finally, the ships sailed away and Lady Franklin later wrote to Ross: "We often look back on the days that you and Captain Crozier were with us, considering them the happiest we have spent here."

Lady Franklin made a journey to the Australian mainland and at Port Lincoln visited the place where the exploring ship *Investigator* had first sighted land nearly forty years before. She set in motion a plan for a monument to Captain Flinders, dedicated by Franklin, who still revered the memory of his early commander. Later it was erected, and the monument stands on that spot today.

Meanwhile, Montagu, the Colonial Secretary, had been in England, where he was considered quite an authority on Tasmania. As usual, he schemed to advance his own ends. No one knows all that he must have said about the "terrible" way Sir John was running the colony. In any case, when he returned in 1841, the conflict with Franklin grew deeper and more vicious.

Montagu knew that Lady Franklin's influence was keeping him from greater power—even from ruling Tasmania. She had seen through his schemes. If only he could get rid of the Franklins, might he not win the governorship? London certainly thought a great deal of him. He had seen to that.

Montagu's open criticism of Lady Franklin had worn Franklin's patience almost to the breaking point. When, at last, Montagu wrote a disrespectful letter to Sir John —accusing him of poor judgment—Franklin reviewed Montagu's actions over the previous months and concluded that there could no longer be any confidence between the Colonial Secretary and himself. Therefore, he suspended Montagu from office.

"After the most anxious and deliberate reflection upon the tone of that Officer's late correspondence," Franklin wrote to London, "and the tenor of his conduct during the last three months, I have arrived at the painful conviction that Mr. Montagu's continuance in the Office of Colonial Secretary would be derogatory to the honour of the crown and detrimental to the Public Service."

A short time afterward, Montagu sailed for England, but the Franklins knew it would not be the last they would hear from him. He had now been completely humiliated, ruined, run out of his country. In London he had friends. He would get even.

After the deed was done, Franklin felt a great relief and pitched into his work with a new confidence. In the spring of 1842 he and Lady Franklin led an exploring expedition from Hobart past Lake St. Clair to Macquarie Harbor. As he climbed and rode over the rocky crags, Sir John felt the wind and rain and sleet in his face. The spirit of exploration came back to him, clearing his mind, renewing his sense of peace and happiness.

When the going became rough and hazardous, Franklin was there to cheer the members of the expedition: "Come, come my boys! This is nothing at all. You should laugh at this!"

They came to a rapid stream, flowing beneath high and often perpendicular banks, overhung with myrtle and pine. One of the members of the party named it Franklin River, "well deserving its honoured and honorable name," he said. Over flooded rivers, muddy flats, slippery slopes of rock, and through dark forests, in constantly foul weather, they journeyed across the wilderness of Tasmania.

Finally they arrived at Macquarie Harbor, where they were met by a ship. But then the weather worsened and they had to wait three weeks before they could sail.

Meanwhile, worry gripped the residents of Hobart. Searchers spread out to look for the governor and his party. Among the vessels joining the hunt was a famed exploring ship, the *Beagle,* which six years earlier had brought a young and unknown scientist named Charles Darwin briefly to Tasmania.

The party was duly rescued, and Tasmanians rejoiced when their governor and his lady returned to Hobart.

The joy did not last long.

A letter arrived from Lord Stanley, Secretary of the Colonial Office in London. "I have received the series of dispatches," it began, "reporting the various occurrences which led to the suspension from office of Mr. Montagu . . . and to the arrival of that Gentleman in this country."

As Franklin read on, his surprise turned into shock. Stanley took up each of the accusations made against Montagu, and on nearly every one he lauded Montagu and concluded that Franklin had been in the wrong.

"The result of my consideration of the whole subject is, as you will see, to relieve Mr. Montagu from every censure which impugns the integrity or the propriety of his conduct . . ."

Not censure him? Was Stanley mad? Montagu must certainly have spread a tale of woe in London. He must have convinced the Colonial Office that Franklin was a governor of the worst sort. The facts were plain. If Montagu's guilt had been erased, then this dispatch was a censure of Franklin himself!

Stanley left no doubt of it. He said that Montagu was as well-thought-of as ever by Her Majesty's Government and though it would be improper for him to return to Tasmania, he had been given a similar post at the Cape of Good Hope, in Africa.

Then Stanley remarked that he wished to hear no more of the matter, and ended his letter with a devastating sentence: "Reluctant as I am to employ a single expression which is likely to be unwelcome to you, I am compelled to add that your proceedings in the case of

Mr. Montagu do not appear to me to have been well-judged; and that your suspension of him from office is not, in my opinion, sufficiently vindicated."

Franklin was numbed, hurt, heartbroken. A lifetime of honorable service had ended in a disgrace that was completely undeserved.

He now had no choice; he asked to be recalled to England. He did not know what he would do. With his life a failure and his future ruined, what hope would there be? He wrote to the Admiralty that he would like to resume his naval work. But after all this, what would they think of him?

He did not leave his post officially, or vacate Government House, until his successor walked up the steps. This was on August 17, 1843, nearly a year after Stanley's letter of censure had been written.

Not long afterward, the Franklins sailed from Launceston.

But it was certainly not in disgrace that he left Tasmania. Six years before, when he first rode into Launceston, the residents met him with a petition of welcome signed by more than three hundred people. Now a farewell statement addressed to him and to Lady Franklin contained the signatures of a thousand persons.

On the day the Franklins departed, an eyewitness described the scene:

"Sir John was dressed in full uniform as a captain in the Royal Navy, and wore the stars of the several orders which have been conferred upon him for distinguished services rendered to his country and the cause of scientific discovery.

"He halted occasionally for an instant to acknowledge the enthusiastic cheers which burst forth from the assembled multitude. The procession was swelled by new arrivals at every step, the cheering being renewed at intervals as the moving mass received fresh accessions.

"Handkerchiefs were waved from verandahs and open windows along the line of route, and there were few who felt entirely unmoved at the scene before them, a loyal and generous people paying a heartfelt tribute of affection to a truly good man with whom their destinies had been bound up for years . . .

"As those near him retired, numbers took their places, and anxiety was visible on every face once again to touch his hand. So many were the crowds succeeding crowds anxious for this last honour that there was a considerable delay.

"At length the signal was given, the oars fell into the water, the battery fired a salute of thirteen guns, a cheer burst from the assembled multitude and was echoed back from the shipping and the boats, which filled with spectators and crowded to accompany him to the vessel. Sir John Franklin bowed his acknowledgments, and the barge, surrounded by a perfect flotilla" of ships, pulled away from shore and headed for the ship in the harbor that was to take him home. "Thus departed from among us as true and upright a ruler as ever the interests of a British colony were entrusted to."

Sir John and Lady Franklin may have thought they left in disgrace. But the Tasmania to which they gave museums, schools, and scientific institutions, and to which they gave seven years of work devoted to the welfare of the imprisoned and the free would honor them forever.

Today a statue of Franklin stands in Franklin Square, the main square of Hobart. His name—and memory— are enshrined in the names of an electoral district, a river, a mountain, and two villages in Tasmania.

Left: Statue of Sir John Franklin, in Franklin Square, Hobart, Tasmania;
Below: Village of Franklin, in Tasmania

Twenty-two

EREBUS AND TERROR

The moment he landed in England in 1844, Sir John went to work to set matters right and to clear his name. To some extent he succeeded. Lord Stanley wrote to him: "I do not doubt that during your administration of Van Diemen's Land your best endeavours were applied to the honest and faithful discharge of your duties, and certainly nothing came under my notice which could in any way derogate from your high character for honour and integrity."

But that was not enough for Franklin. It did not erase the rebuke he had received for suspending Montagu. Still hurt, still angry, still feeling that his side of the story had never been heard, Franklin wrote and published the story of his experiences in Van Diemen's Land.

But the quarrel was soon overshadowed by events.

Even before Franklin had gone to Van Diemen's Land, the Royal Geographical Society had petitioned the government to make new attempts to solve the remaining mysteries of the Arctic. They had asked for Franklin's advice and he had written: "You know, I am sure, that no service is nearer my heart than the completion of the survey of the north coast of America and the accomplishment of a Northwest Passage."

His eagerness had never diminished in all his years in

Tasmania. And in those years there had been a little progress in Arctic exploration. Sir Edward Parry had pushed through Lancaster Sound and Barrow's Strait as far west as the 114th meridian. Two officers of the Hudson's Bay Company—Peter Dease and Thomas Simpson—had explored the 160 miles of northern Alaska coast that had separated Beechey's and Franklin's expeditions in 1826. They had also mapped beyond Point Turnagain, the farthest east that Franklin had reached in 1821.

By now all indications were that a channel through the northern islands did exist. But where exactly? All that remained was to connect the last few hundred miles and see if the ice ever melted enough to let ships through. The merchants of Europe still clung to the hope that a short route to China could be found. Even if it could be used only in summer, that would help immensely.

Once again the people and the government recalled how much of the search for the Northwest Passage had already been done by Englishmen. If another country—using English maps—were to make the final discovery!

Impossible! cried Admiral Sir Francis Beaufort. England should have the honor of forging the last link. "It would be an intolerable disgrace to this country," he said, "were the flag of any other nation to be borne through it before our own."

Britain must not be robbed of her discoveries, said Sir John Barrow. She must not let another nation pass through a door which she herself had opened.

As a result of this renewal of interest, a Northwest Passage Expedition was organized. To command it, the Admiralty gave first choice to Franklin's old friend, Sir James Ross. It was the right choice, simply because Ross at that time—1845—had more Polar experience than

Portrait of Sir John Franklin, photographed from a painting by Negelin anyone. He had been on seven expeditions. He was in good health, not too old, and an excellent leader.

But Ross declined. He knew that the only man alive who deserved the honor of commanding this voyage was Franklin, and the Royal Society agreed. Now it was up to the Admiralty.

On February 5, 1845, Franklin met with Lord Haddington, First Lord of the Admiralty.

"I say, Sir John," said Lord Haddington, "have you thought seriously of the nature of this undertaking—at your age? For, you know, I know your age. You are 59."

"Not quite, sir."

"Can your body bear it?"

"You'll examine me."

Lord Haddington frowned. "Come, Franklin. I have a great responsibility in this."

"I realize that, your Lordship."

"You are already a hero—a hero to the world. If you broke down on this expedition, I would be reproached for having appointed so old a fellow."

"My experience, sir . . ."

"I know all your services, Sir John. They have been arduous ones, from an early age. And now you have just returned from a civil service in Van Diemen's Land that must have caused you great care and anxiety."

A trace of a smile appeared on Franklin's face. "The anxieties of an expedition, sir, are not equal to those of a governorship."

"I am thinking of bodily wear and tear," Lord Haddington replied. "I cannot conceive of anything more trying than several years in the Arctic. Certainly time has weakened *my* body. Everyone knows how difficult your

Canadian trips have been, and how you got through them. But . . . you are not as young as you once were."

"I must beg your Lordship to understand that if I did not think myself equal to it, I should not wish to go. Dr. Richardson has declared my fitness."

"I want no other person's testimony—only your own."

"If this were a *walking* expedition, my Lord, I should not undertake it. I am much stouter than I was before. In a ship, it is different."

Lord Haddington paused for a moment. Then he said slowly: "This requires a little consideration. In a day or two you will hear from me."

Lady Franklin sympathized with her husband. She was worried, too. She knew his age. She also knew his ambition. In a letter to Sir James Ross she pointed out that Franklin had been deeply hurt by the unfair censure he had received from Lord Stanley. If his own department, the Navy, didn't have confidence in him any more, she said, that would be even worse. She dreaded the effect on his mind if he were refused command of the expedition.

Sir Edward Parry, when asked by Lord Haddington about Franklin's ability to command the expedition, said: "If you don't let him go, the man will die of disappointment."

But he was not to be disappointed. On February 7, 1845, Franklin learned that the Admiralty had appointed him commander of the expedition.

How his spirits rose! At the Admiralty he pointed eagerly to a map of northern Canada.

"There!" he said, his finger on the western entrance of Simpson Strait. "If I can but get down there, my work is done. From there it will be plain sailing to the west-ward."

The ships assigned to the expedition were famous ones—the *Erebus* and *Terror*—and familiar ones to Franklin. Ross and Crozier had brought them to Tasmania and had gone to the Antarctic in them. Before that, George Back had sailed the *Terror* to Hudson's Bay and back.

Both ships had been completely repaired and fitted with that strange new method of propulsion—steam power. Each had a screw propeller—the first time the screw, as a means of propelling a ship, would be used in the Arctic. And each had a steam engine that could work up twenty horsepower at its peak of energy. That wasn't much but it might make all the difference at some disastrous moment when the wind failed and they could not use sails to flee the crushing ice.

Franklin took command of the *Erebus,* with Commander James Fitzjames as his second officer. To sail the *Terror,* Franklin selected his old friend, Captain Crozier.

Public interest in the expedition became so high that applications arrived from hundreds of men who wanted to go. Finally, the 134 men of the expedition were chosen and loaded aboard the ships.

"I wish that you could see the ship now, "Franklin wrote in a letter. "The officers and the crew are all fine young men in excellent spirits. This day we had the happiness of joining together on board in Divine worship, to praise God for His past mercies and to implore His guiding and protecting providence. In this spirit we all hope to begin, continue, and end our voyage."

On May 19, 1845, the *Erebus* and *Terror,* accompanied by transport ships with extra supplies, departed from England.

Out across the Atlantic the little squadron sailed. In the two main ships were crammed supplies of every sort to last three years in the icy wilderness. No doubt the happiest of all the crew was the commander. Captain Fitzjames wrote:

"Sir John is delightful, active, and energetic. What he *has*

Some of Franklin's officers: *Top, from left to right:* **Mr. Couch (mate), Lt. Fairholme, C. H. Osmer (purser), Mr. Des Voeux (mate);** *Bottom from left to right:* **Capt. Crozier ("Terror"), Lt. Graham Gore, Commander Fitzjames, J. Stanley (surgeon)**

been, we all know. I think it will turn out that he is in no ways altered. He is full of conversation and interesting anecdotes of his former voyages. I would not lose him for the command, for I have a real regard, I might say affection, for him, and believe this is felt by all of us . . .

"I like a man who is earnest. Sir John Franklin read the church service today and a sermon so very beautifully that I defy any man not to feel the force of what he would convey."

In stormy seas the ships rounded Cape Farewell, on the southern tip of Greenland, and anchored in the Whale Fish Islands. Here they replenished their supplies from the transports that had accompanied them.

Franklin sat by candlelight in his cabin at night and wrote to his wife. Most of all he urged her not to worry if the expedition failed to return after that first winter.

"It is very possible, that our prospects of success and the health of our officers and men might justify our passing a second winter in these regions. If we do not succeed in our attempt, we shall try in other places, and through God's blessing we hope to set the question at rest . . .

"To the Almighty care I commit you and dear Eleanor. I trust He will shield you under His wings and grant the continual aid of His Holy Spirit. Again, that God may bless and support you both is and will be the constant prayer of your most affectionate husband . . ."

On July 10, 1845, the *Erebus* and *Terror* raised anchors, loosed braces, and sailed northward toward Melville Bay. There they were seen by a whaling ship whose captain reported the crews all well and in good spirits, anchored beside an iceberg, making observations, and expecting to finish their voyage in excellent time.

Then the whaling ship left, and the Franklin expedition sailed toward Lancaster Sound.

Twenty-three

THE SEARCH

England waited. The world waited.

All during 1845 and 1846 there was no word. There was not much worry either. Other things were occupying people's minds: The Americans were fighting a war with Mexico, and the floor of the Atlantic Ocean was being studied to see if a transoceanic telegraph cable could be laid across it.

Lady Franklin bravely bore the pain of separation from her husband, knowing what he was doing for science and exploration. She tried to tell herself that there was not the slightest reason to worry. John had, after all, expected that the ships might spend a second winter in the Arctic.

By the summer of 1847, however, there was still no word. Anxiety began to spread across the nation. The Hudson's Bay Company ordered special stocks of food and supplies taken to its northern posts. Should any of the members of the expedition straggle across the frozen wastes, half-starved, they would at least find food waiting for them. Franklin knew what it was to starve. No one wanted that to happen to him again.

Officials alerted the Indians in northern Canada to watch for the party, to help the men when found, and to report any contact immediately. The English government offered rewards to anyone who would bring back news of the expedition.

But with each passing month, Lady Franklin's anxiety deepened. She herself offered a reward of £2,000 (then about $10,000) for information about the fate of the expedition.

When 1848 arrived—three years after the *Erebus* and *Terror* had sailed—the world still had no word. Not a clue came back from the silent Arctic. Not even a rumor. Nothing.

Anxiety turned into concern, and concern into action. If something had happened to the ships a year or two before, it might already be too late. But rescue must be started. Relief must be sent to Franklin, wherever he and his men might be, and quickly.

But this was easier said than done. Where would the rescue ships begin to search in a land so vast and little known? The many islands of northern Canada lay scattered in seeming disarray across the Arctic landscape. Worse yet, the bays and sounds and passages in that day were imperfectly known.

When the Arctic Council, a group of veteran explorers including Parry, Ross, Richardson, Beechey, and Back, met to consider how the search should be conducted, it knew that the problem was enormous. The officers had to reexamine Franklin's original plans, making sure they knew where he had intended to go. Then they had to figure out which of the hundreds of directions he could have gone instead, depending on weather and ice conditions.

What if Melville Sound were frozen? Where would the *Erebus* and *Terror* go then? Down Prince Regent Inlet? That was a possibility. Up Wellington Channel?

That, too, was possible. Faced with such vast territory to search, and under such uncertainties, the Admiralty decided to send as many vessels as could be equipped to investigate the greatest number of routes.

The first expedition to depart left England in June, 1848, under Franklin's old friend, Sir James Ross. He

The Arctic Council planning the search for Sir John Franklin. Franklin's portrait is hanging at left; the portrait in the middle is of Capt. James Fitzjames, who commanded the *Erebus* as second in command under Franklin, and the portrait at the right is of Sir John Barrow. The National Portrait Gallery in London lists the persons in the Council as follows *(left to right):* Sir George Back, Sir William E. Parry, Capt. Edward J. Bird; Sir James Clark Ross, Sir Francis Beaufort *(seated),* John Barrow, Lt. Col. Sabine, Capt. W. A. Baillie Hamilton, Sir John Richardson, Capt. Frederick William Beechey *(seated).* (From the painting by Stephen Pearce)

steered his ships, the *Enterprise* and *Investigator,* directly toward Canada. Accompanying Ross was a young and enthusiastic, dark-haired officer named Leopold McClintock. As the journey progressed, McClintock stored up an extraordinary amount of knowledge and information about the Arctic.

The second expedition, commanded by Sir John Richardson, Franklin's friend and traveling companion of earlier journeys, left for Canada to approach the Polar Sea by familiar overland routes. With this expedition went a sturdy young Scot, an Orkney Islander named John Rae, an official of the Hudson's Bay Company. He, too, was destined to make some critical discoveries.

Sir James Ross and his ships got no farther west than Peel Sound and had to return in 1849 without a trace of the missing expedition. Richardson hunted desperately along the route he knew so well—down the Mackenzie River and east along the edge of the Polar Sea to the mouth of the Coppermine River. But when he returned to England, he could only report: no sign of Franklin anywhere. His companion, John Rae, had stayed on in the Arctic to continue the search—without luck.

The whole nation was alarmed by now. A complete expedition—two ships and 134 men—was missing. The government offered a reward of £20,000, and Lady Franklin another £3,800 to anyone who would find and help the lost explorers. The people prayed for the men and contributed money toward the search.

In faraway Tasmania, people in churches and chapels offered special public prayers for the governor who had served them so well and won their hearts. The colonists collected £1,700 which were sent to Lady Franklin to help carry on the hunt.

£20,000
REWARD

WILL BE GIVEN BY

Her Majesty's Government

TO ANY PARTY OR PARTIES, OF ANY COUNTRY, WHO SHALL RENDER EFFICIENT
ASSISTANCE TO THE CREWS OF THE

DISCOVERY SHIPS

UNDER THE COMMAND OF

SIR JOHN FRANKLIN,

1.—To any Party or Parties who, in the judgment of the
Board of Admiralty, shall discover and effectually relieve the
Crews of Her Majesty's Ships "Erebus" and "Terror," the
Sum of

£20,000.

OR

2. To any Party or Parties who, in the judgment of the
Board of Admiralty, shall discover and effectually relieve *any*
of the Crews of Her Majesty's Ships "Erebus" and "Terror,"
or shall convey such intelligence as shall lead to the relief of
such Crews or *any* of them, the Sum of

£10,000.

OR

3.—To any Party or Parties who, in the judgment of the
Board of Admiralty, shall by virtue of his or their efforts first
succeed in ascertaining their fate,

£10,000.

W. A. B. HAMILTON,

Secretary of the Admiralty

Admiralty, March 7th, 1850.

Franklin Reward poster, issued in 1850

In 1850, the *Enterprise* and *Investigator* went out again, under command of Captain Richard Collinson, and this time entered the Polar Sea from the Pacific side, around Alaska and through the Bering Strait. In the *Investigator*, Commander Robert McClure found two channels leading to seas that had already been explored from the Atlantic side. These were, in fact, two "northwest passages," and McClure is often credited with discovery of the true Northwest Passage. He and his crew were awarded £10,000 by Parliament for being the first navigators ever to cross from the Pacific to the Atlantic Ocean by way of the coast of North America.

However, McClure's route was not an open one. His vessel had been frozen in the pack and had to be left behind when he and his men were rescued by explorers from the east. His route, even though an actual channel of ice, was not the route Franklin sought and hence not the true Northwest Passage later navigated by ship.

Not long after McClure's voyage, Captain Horatio Austin led a squadron of four ships into Lancaster Sound. Elsewhere, every whaling ship in the Arctic regions was ordered to keep on the lookout and search as best it could.

Even the people of the United States became alarmed. A New York merchant, Henry Grinnell, fitted out an expedition that was manned by officers and seamen of the U.S. Navy. These men sailed as fast as they could to help their British friends around Lancaster Sound.

Lady Franklin, whose own anxieties by now must have been almost unbearable, equipped and staffed a 90-ton schooner and dispatched it to search the shores of Prince Regent Inlet. Even Sir John Ross, uncle of Sir James Ross, took a schooner and a yacht into the pack and, despite the fact that he was 74 years old, helped in the hunt for his long-lost friend.

By the end of 1850 the search for Franklin had become one of the largest rescue operations in history. There were fifteen vessels directly engaged in this service, with millions of people praying for their success.

The first discovery of any sort was made by Captain Austin in Barrow Strait. On a lonely and desolate frozen isle called Beechey Island, he found three graves. Together with other evidence, these indicated that the Franklin expedition had camped there for a while, most likely during the winter of 1845 and 1846.

It was meager evidence, but it was a clue at last. As for the rest of Captain Austin's searches, and those of all the other ships engaged in the search, new geographic discoveries were made, new observations taken, and many a new adventure tale was brought back to thrill the world—but not one other trace of the lost ships or their crews was found.

The question was, with all those rescue vessels in the Arctic, how could they *miss* the lost expedition? Frustration gripped the nation—and Lady Franklin most of all. With each of the searching parties she sent devoted letters to Sir John, hoping against hope that they would be delivered. All came back.

In 1851 she sent a schooner named *Prince Albert* back to explore Prince Regent Inlet, convinced that Franklin must have turned in that direction. This expedition discovered Bellot Strait—which separates the Boothia Peninsula from Somerset Island—but no *Erebus*, no *Terror*, and no survivors.

If any of Franklin's men were alive, at this late date, it would be a miracle. Without food or clothing, their chances would be slim indeed. Men do not last long in the Arctic unless they live with Eskimos—but that might have happened. No doubt by now the ships had been crushed in ice or slammed ashore and wrecked.

Nevertheless, dead or alive, the men must be somewhere. Dead or alive, every one of them was a hero and the English have a way with heroes. They knew that they owed it to the memory of Franklin and his men to keep on searching until they found out what had happened.

In 1852, the Admiralty promoted Franklin, *in absentia,* to the rank of Admiral. That same year, Lady Franklin dispatched the screw steamer *Isabel* to continue the search.

The government refitted four ships that had previously gone out under Captain Austin and sent them forth under Sir Edward Belcher. Again, one of the captains was Leopold McClintock, whose store of Arctic knowledge was growing larger. The men of this expedition searched Melville, Prince Patrick, Bathurst and other islands—by ship, by sledge, and afoot. They laboriously sailed their ships into Wellington and other channels. They hacked at the ice and fled from dangerous streams of icebergs. For two winters they lay locked in the frozen seas and finally had to abandon every one of their vessels and return to England in the ships of another expedition.

One of the abandoned vessels, the *Resolute,* ultimately wandered by itself—floating on water and riding ice floes—out through Lancaster Sound to Baffin Bay and down into Davis Strait where it was found by an American whaling ship. Could something like that have happened to the *Erebus* or the *Terror?* The Arctic has strange ways . . .

Another schooner from the United States was sent

out by Henry Grinnell, this one under command of Dr. Elisha Kent Kane. In 1853 it sailed north into Smith's Sound and wintered at latitude 78 degrees—nearer the Pole than any ship had wintered before. This was so far north, in fact, that the ice never melted during the entire next summer. Kane and his starving men had to abandon their ships and make a perilous trip in smaller boats to settlements in Greenland. In all this time they heard and found no clue to the Franklin party.

The same year that Kane went north from the United States, Dr. John Rae was sent into the Arctic by the Hudson's Bay Company. The following year he met some Eskimos in Pelly Bay and asked the questions that had been asked by now a thousand times in the Arctic: had they seen any white men in the last few years?

This time the answer was different.

Yes, the Indians replied, they had seen some white men.

How many?

A party of about forty.

What were they doing?

Traveling south, dragging sledges and a boat.

What did they look like?

They were very thin. They were also very hungry. None spoke Eskimo, but they indicated that their ships had been destroyed by ice. They were going overland hunting food. They fell down and died as they walked along.

Where did they go?

Toward the Great Fish River.

Did anyone see the ships?

Yes. There was a body in one of them.

What else?

Dr. John Rae

The Eskimos produced silver spoons, forks, and other objects that were, beyond question, the property of the ill-fated explorers.

Rae also wrote:

"The corpses of some thirty persons, and some graves, were discovered on the continent, and five dead bodies on an island near it, about a long day's journey to the N.W. of the mouth of a large stream, which can be no other than Back's Great Fish River . . .

"Some of the bodies were in a tent, or tents; others were under the boat, which had been turned over to form a shelter, and some lay scattered about in different directions. Of those seen on the island, it was supposed that one was that of an officer (chief), as he had a telescope strapped over his shoulders, and a double-barrelled gun lay underneath him.

"From the mutilated state of many of the bodies, and the contents of the kettles, it is evident that our wretched countrymen had been driven to the dread alternative of cannibalism as a means of sustaining life. A few of the unfortunate men must have survived until the arrival of the wild fowl . . . as shots were heard and fresh bones and feathers of geese were noticed near the scene of the sad event."

When news of this discovery got to England, there was relief as well as sorrow. After all these years, and all these voyages, someone had found eye-witnesses to the fate of the expedition.

For some people, that solved the matter. It satisfied the Admiralty. As far as they were concerned, the *Erebus* and *Terror* had obviously been frozen in ice for more than one winter, as some of the rescue ships had been. Provisions ran low. The men began to starve. Some, at least, had tried to go overland. Others remained in the ships and probably a number of them had died aboard and been buried at sea. One thing was sure: none could be alive. Not now. It was 1854, nine years since Franklin and his crews had last been seen.

And so the government decided to consider the expedition lost, the crews dead, the matter closed. More rescue expeditions, it announced, would simply be a waste of time and money and probably lives. No further government trips would be authorized.

But the public was not at all satisfied. Most assuredly Lady Franklin was not. Had even a single written record of the expedition been found? Not at all. There was only the word of Eskimos. Who knew the fate of Sir John himself, or—save for the graves on Beechey Island—of the remaining crewmen unaccounted for? There must be other proof, somewhere, deep in the snow perhaps, or hidden beneath a cairn . . .

People in England and elsewhere clamored for additional searches. Since the Eskimos had informed Dr. Rae that the lost men they had seen were heading toward the Great Fish River, an expedition was sent out by the Hudson's Bay Company in 1855 to search there. Not a thing was discovered.

Lady Franklin was now exasperated in the extreme. Repeatedly she begged the Admiralty to resume the search. To everyone who would listen she pleaded for the government to send another expedition.

During 1856 a petition, signed by Arctic officers and eminent scientists, urged the authorities to continue the search in order "to satisfy the honour of our country and clear up a mystery which has excited the sympathy of the civilized world."

It did no good. The government refused again.

Lady Franklin resolved to take matters once more into her own hands. Aided by private funds, but mostly with the use of her own, she purchased and equipped a small steam yacht called the *Fox*. It was a little ship, scarcely 170 tons burthen, expected to accomplish what powerful ships of the English Navy had already failed to do. Furthermore, when it finally sailed, it was manned by a crew of only twenty-six.

Regardless of size, reckoned Lady Franklin, any ship would succeed if it went to the right place. With all the information that had been accumulated from other vessels, the area of search was very much narrowed. At least they knew where *not* to look.

To command her little vessel she selected Captain Mc-Clintock, whose experience made him one of the best qualified to search for Franklin. For his second in command he chose a young officer named W. R. Hobson, who had also distinguished himself in the Arctic.

Provisions for nearly two and a half years were packed into the little ship and, on the first of July, 1857, she sailed toward the Polar Sea. Somewhere, her captain was convinced, lay a record of the lost expedition. God willing, they would find it and solve a riddle whose answer the world was waiting for.

Twenty-four

DISCOVERY

All went well until the little ship arrived in Melville Bay. Here the *Fox* was frozen in the pack, and all that winter she drifted as the pack ice drifted.

By the spring of 1858, when the ice had melted and loosed its grip on the yacht, she had drifted nearly 1,200 miles to the south. McClintock and his crew were sorely vexed by this setback, but as soon as the ship was free, they steered her once again for the Polar Sea.

This time they were more successful, and that summer they got all the way through Lancaster Sound. At Beechey Island they erected a marble tablet sent by Lady Franklin to mark the spot where the *Erebus* and *Terror* had first wintered.

Leaving Beechey Island, McClintock encountered solid ice to the west, and so turned south into Prince Regent Inlet. It was just as well. That would get him closer to the two main places he wanted to explore: King William Island and the mouth of the Great Fish River. He well remembered what the Eskimos at Pelly Bay had told Dr. Rae five years before about the survivors of the expedition. McClintock meant to find out more from the Eskimos and to have a look at the land in that vicinity.

The little *Fox*, fighting its way through Prince Regent Inlet, was hardly a match for the ponderous icebergs coming in streams through the icy sea. The tiny craft was almost constantly in danger. Only through daring and desperation, and extremely hard work, was the crew able to keep it afloat. The ship was caught between great masses of ice, which crashed together forward or aft as the vessel careened along. Once the ice bore it to within two hundred yards of the rocky shore.

In Bellot Strait, great whirlpools and dangerously violent currents tossed the vessel like a chip on a stormy sea. Three times they tried to navigate the strait and finally did—only to find that the sea beyond was clogged with ice.

Looking carefully at this "western sea," McClintock knew that Franklin must have sailed it—and the only way he knew that was from the slender evidence that Dr. Rae had found near Great Fish River. If Franklin and his men had gotten to that river, they must have come through the strait now frozen in front of him.

"It has been navigated by Franklin only," McClintock wrote in his book, *The Fate of Sir John Franklin,* "and by him proved to be a strait. I have deemed it due to that distinguished man to designate it 'Sir John Franklin Strait.' "

This passage is still called Franklin Strait. In fact, though McClintock could not have known it then, the entire archipelago of Arctic islands of northern Canada, covering more than half a million square miles, would some day be known as the District of Franklin. Perhaps even McClintock could not in 1858 have guessed how many Arctic features would be named after the man for whom he searched: Cape Franklin, Fort Franklin, the Franklin Mountains, Franklin Bay, Franklin Island, Franklin Lake, and Point Franklin. There would also be

Lady Franklin Point, Lady Franklin Bay, Cape Jane Franklin, and Cape Lady Franklin.

Back in the eastern end of Bellot Strait, McClintock and his intrepid crew established winter quarters and began at once to plan their explorations over the ice. As soon as the sun should appear in February, a group on sledges would travel toward the North Magnetic Pole and try to contact the Eskimos again. Another would set up forward supply posts on Prince of Wales Island.

So they set out, early in 1859, with the temperature at forty below zero. Near the magnetic pole McClintock met the Eskimos and they produced some spoons, forks, naval uniform buttons, and a silver medal that belonged to the assistant surgeon of the *Terror*. None of the Eskimos had seen the ships or their crews, though one had seen bones of white men on an island where they had died.

An island! McClintock remembered Rae's information from other Eskimos. The story was almost the same. He had to find that island. He carefully studied his maps. The island, the one not fully explored as yet, seemed to be King William Island—at the mouth of Franklin Strait.

Returning to the *Fox* after an absence of nearly four weeks and a distance of 360 miles, McClintock ordered immediate preparations for the sledges to leave for the south. He was sure now that he was on the right trail.

Two parties made ready—one under McClintock, the other under Lieutenant Hobson. Each consisted of a sledge pulled by four men, and a dog sledge with driver. Each was provisioned for almost three months.

Bidding goodby to their companions, who were to remain at winter quarters, they left the *Fox* on April 2, 1859 and proceeded southward along the west coast of the Boothia Peninsula. Arriving at Cape Victoria, they

**Sir Leopold McClintock, from a painting
by Stephen Pearce**

separated. McClintock headed for the Great Fish River,
Hobson started on his way around King William Island.

Hobson was puzzled. He knew that the best chance of
discovery lay upon King William Island. Why had Mc-
Clintock not reserved the island for himself? Why was he

offering his lieutenant the honors of discovery that all of them sought?

McClintock admitted that he had been searching for Franklin for all these years, and that Lady Franklin had engaged him to command this expedition.

Then why? Hobson could not understand.

Because, McClintock said, he was getting on in years and had already succeeded well enough in life. If this expedition made any discoveries he would be properly honored for commanding it. On the other hand, Hobson was young. If he were to make a big discovery, it would mean fame and recognition in his growing career.

And so the route of search was fixed. They wished each other good fortune and then departed.

The Eskimos had told them that two vessels had been seen by the people of King William Island. One had been crushed by ice and sunk; the other had come ashore and been wrecked. Consequently, McClintock and Hobson kept careful watch for any remains of a lost ship, or indeed for anything that might have washed ashore. And again they heard that some white men had journeyed with a boat toward the Great Fish River.

Sledging as fast as they could under heavy loads, McClintock and his men crossed James Ross Strait and proceeded along the eastern coast of King William Island. They came to a village where thirty or forty Eskimos lived and from them got some pieces of silver plate that bore the crests or initials of Franklin, Crozier, and others of the missing expedition.

These Indians said that on the west coast of King William Island, five days' march away, lay a wrecked ship, but that little of it remained. Were there any books or papers? McClintock asked, trying to describe things to the natives that they probably had never seen before.

Yes, came the answer, but all these things had long ago been ruined by ice and snow and were lost.

McClintock and his men continued their journey toward the mouth of the Great Fish River. They knew very well that they might be treading on important evidence they could not see because of the cover of snow. But he could not wait until the snow melted. By summer they must return to the *Fox* and start on their way to England. Already they had gathered a great deal of information and had purchased some relics of the lost expedition.

As fast as they could, they explored Montreal Island, at the mouth of the Great Fish River, but found nothing. Crossing over to the mainland and back to King William Island, they came upon a human skeleton lying face down in the snow near Cape Herschel. The bones were bleached and, from the clothing still attached, they assumed that it was the corpse of an officer's steward. Nothing else.

At the westernmost point of King William Island, which McClintock named Cape Crozier after the second in command of the ill-fated expedition, the little group turned to the northwest. The following morning, May 30, they found a boat that had been mounted on a sledge.

The boat, some 28 feet in length, was worn by weather and was falling to pieces. Inside they found two human skeletons. One was apparently that of a young man, slightly built. The other was of a large and strongly built person, possibly an officer.

Carefully searching the boat, McClintock found a number of books, mostly religious, five watches, two double-barreled guns (loaded, cocked, and ready to fire), clothing, and a little tea and chocolate. That was all. No names. No messages. No records.

It was obvious now that Franklin's ships had come through Peel Sound in the summer of 1846 and had been trapped in the ice in Franklin Strait—somewhere off the coast of King William Island. Furthermore, the ice must not have melted enough in 1847 to free the ships, whereupon the men abandoned the *Erebus* and *Terror* and started south. They built big sledges on which to haul their boats so as to navigate sea or lakes or streams.

But what astonished McClintock was that the sledge on which the boat was fastened pointed north, the way in which they were traveling. He wrote:

"A little reflection led me to satisfy my own mind at least that this boat was *returning to the ships*. In no other way can I account for two men having been left in her, than by supposing the party were unable to drag the boat further, and that these two men, not being able to keep pace with their shipmates, were therefore left by them supplied with such provisions as could be spared, to last them until the return of the others from the ship with a fresh stock . . .

"Whether all or any of the remainder of this detached party ever reached their ships is uncertain; all we know is, that they did not revisit the boat, otherwise more skeletons would probably have been found in its neighborhood; the Esquimaux report that there was no one alive in the ship when she drifted on shore, and that they found but one human body on board of her . . .

"I need hardly say that throughout the whole of my journey along the shores of King William's Land, we all kept a most vigilant look-out for any appearance of the stranded ship spoken of by the natives; but our search for her was utterly fruitless."

It was while he explored King William Island that McClintock came to a cairn in which Lieutenant Hobson had left a note. Hobson had made the most important discovery of all.

Twenty-five

NORTHWEST PASSAGE

Lieutenant Hobson, sledging down the west coast of King William Island, discovered a number of cairns and other relics of the lost expedition. But it was at Victory Point that he found what he was looking for.

As the lieutenant and his men worked their way up the ridge toward the cairn they had sighted from afar, their hopes must have risen again. Could it be that here, fourteen years after the expedition had sailed from England, was a record of its fate? Could it be that on this lonely point lay the evidence that nearly forty expeditions had hunted in the past eleven years?

The men stumbled to the top of the ridge. Their eyes widened. Before them, strewn about the cairn, lay piles of equipment that appeared to have been discarded by men who were leaving this point and could take little with them.

Hobson and his men carefully examined every fragment of evidence. They found cooking stoves, pickaxes, shovels, iron hoops, canvas, curtain rods, a medicine case containing about 24 bottles of perfectly preserved medicines, and some nautical and magnetic instruments.

The clothing lay in a pile four feet high. Every scrap of it was searched, but not one piece was marked and not a thing could be found in any of the pockets.

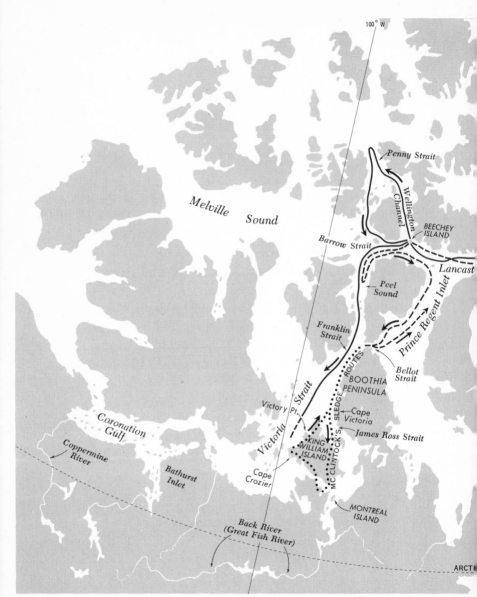

Franklin's last voyage (solid line); McClintock's search expedition

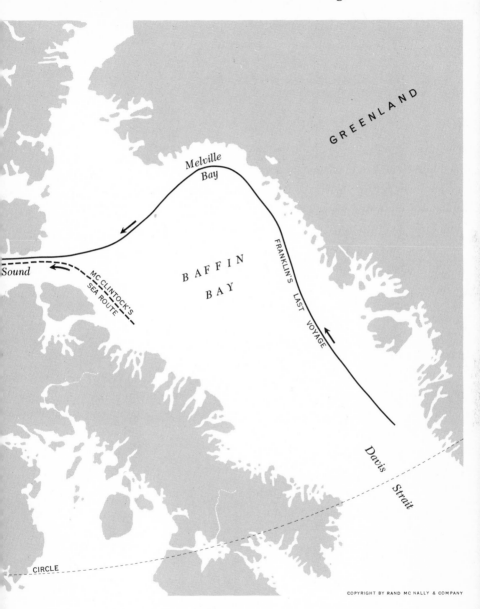

by sea (dashes) and by sledge (dotted line)—in Chapters 24 and 25

The cairn had been built of large and heavy rocks. Some of these had fallen from the top and lay strewn about the base.

"Look!" cried one of the men, rushing forward and snatching a rusty cylinder that lay among the stones. The others came up quickly.

Hobson took the cylinder and turned it over in his mittens. There was a tiny crack in it, which apparently had been soldered tight but then reopened. Peering into the crack, he could see the edge of a paper.

Slowly and carefully, the lieutenant inserted a knife blade into the opening and pried the cylinder open. Inside they saw a graying, crumpled paper that had the appearance of an official document.

The lieutenant took off one of his mittens and, with the utmost care, began to work the paper out of the cylinder. The rusting of the can had caused one corner of the paper to come off, and there were other rust spots on the document. Hobson worked with excruciating slowness, for the paper was old and brittle and even the slightest movement in haste would tear or otherwise damage it. As he unrolled the paper, inch by inch, his breath caught at what he saw.

"A bottle paper!" he gasped.

It was a standard emergency notice issued by the British Admiralty. On it were printed instructions in six languages that requested the finder to forward it to the Secretary of the Admiralty, London, with a note of the time and place at which it was found: or, if more convenient, to deliver it for that purpose to the British Consul at the nearest Port.

The blanks were filled in, and pen and ink writing spilled into the margins. Hobson said: "Look mates! It's dated the 28th of May, 1847, and is signed by Lieutenant Graham Gore . . . and by Charles Des Voeux, Mate of the *Erebus*. It's a record of the Franklin expedition!"

Hobson read aloud: "Her Majesty's Ships *Erebus* and *Terror* wintered in the ice in Latitude 70 degrees five minutes North, Longitude 98 degrees, 23 minutes West. Having wintered in 1846–7 at Beechey Island—"

He stopped, frowning. The other men looked at him.

"The date," Hobson replied. "Something's wrong with the date. I thought they wintered at Beechey Island in the winter of 1845 and '46."

"They did, sir. That's what the gravestones tell us."

"Well," Hobson said, "they dated this paper May 28, 1847, yet they say they wintered way up at Beechey Island that same winter."

"They couldn't have, sir. That's four hundred miles from here."

"I know. If they had wintered at Beechey Island in 1847, they would still have been frozen in the ice there during May, not here where this paper was written."

The graves on Beechey Island

Hobson was thoughtful for a moment. "Lieutenant Gore made a mistake. That's the only answer I can see. He must have meant that they spent their first winter on Beechey Island in 1845 and '46. The following summer they sailed this way, toward King William Island, and spent the *second* winter here."

Hobson went on to read the latitude and longitude of Beechey Island, as written on the paper. "Here now—he says where they went that summer: 'Ascended Wellington Channel to Latitude 77 degrees and returned by the West side of Cornwallis Island. Sir John Franklin commanding the Expedition. All well. Party consisting of 2 officers and 6 men left the ships on Monday 24th May, 1847.' "

He stopped and looked at the faces of his companions. "And then they signed their names."

"But sir, it doesn't say what happened."

"Not up to this point," the lieutenant replied. "When they wrote this, all *was* well. They put the paper in the cylinder and sealed it. But later—they came back . . ."

"Came back? Is there more, sir?"

"Yes, here, around the margin. They apparently returned in great distress, reopened the cylinder and wrote again on the same paper."

Hobson read the paper silently for a few moments. It was not as easy to read as the bold pen strokes of the original entry. It occurred to him that the part he had so far read must have been written on board one of the ships and placed here shortly after.

The remarks by Gore and Des Voeux were routine enough—the kind of information an Arctic explorer would be expected to place in a cairn for the guidance of those who came after him. The writing in the margin must have been done right here—after thawing out the

H. M. S.hips *Erebus and Terror*
{ Wintered in the Ice in

28 of May 1847 { Lat. 70° 5' N Long. 98° 23' W

Having wintered in 1846—7 at Beechey Island

in Lat 74° 43' 28" N. Long 91° 39' 15" W After having

ascended Wellington Channel to Lat 77° and returned

by the West side of Cornwallis Island

_____ Commander.

Sir John Franklin commanding the Expedition

All well

WHOEVER finds this paper is requested to forward it to the Secretary of the Admiralty, London, *with a note of the time and place at which it was found:* or, if more convenient, to deliver it for that purpose to the British Consul at the nearest Port.

QUINCONQUE trouvera ce papier est prié d'y marquer le tems et lieu ou il l'aura trouvé, et de le faire parvenir au phitot au Secretaire de l'Amirauté Britannique à Londres.

CUALQUIERA que hallare este Papel, se lesuplica de enviarlo al Secretario del Almirantazgo, en Londrés, cou una nota del tiempo y del lugar en donde se halló.

EEN ieder die dit Papier mogt vinden, wordt hiermede verzogt, om het zelve, ten spoedigste, te willen zenden aan den Heer Minister van de Marine der Nederlanden in 's Gravenhage, of wel aan den Secretaris der Britsche Admiraliteit, te London, en daar by te voegen eene Nota, inhoudende de tyd en de plaats alwaar dit Papier is gevonden geworden

FINDEREN af dette Papiir ombedes, naar Leilighed gives, at sende samme til Admiralitets Secretairen i London, eller noermeste Embedsmand i Danmark, Norge, eller Sverrig. Tiden og Stoedit hvor dette er fundet önskes venskabelgt paategnet.

WER diesen Zettel findet, wird hier durch ersucht denselben an den Secretair des Admiralitets in London, einzusenden, mit gefälliger angabe an welchen ort und zu welcher zeit er gefundet worden ist.

Party consisting of 2 Officers and 6 Men

left the Ships on Monday 24th May 1847

Gm Gore Lieut

Chas F Des Vaeux Mate

[Marginal notes:]

25th April 1848 HMS Ships Terror and Erebus were deserted on the 22nd April 5 leagues NNW of this having been beset since 12th Sept 1846. The Officers & Crews consisting of 105 souls under the command of Captain F.R.M. Crozier landed here — in Lat 69° 37' 42" Long 98° 41'

This paper was found by Lieut Irving under the cairn supposed to have been built by Sir James Ross in 1831—4 miles to the Northward — where it had been deposited by the late Commander Gore in June 1847. Sir James Ross' pillar has not however been found and the paper has been transferred to this position which is that in which Sir J. Ross' pillar was erected —

Sir John Franklin died on the 11th June 1847 and the total loss by deaths in the Expedition has been to this date 9 Officers & 15 Men

James Fitzjames Captain HMS Erebus

F.R.M. Crozier Captain & Senior Offr

and start on tomorrow 26th for Back's Fish River

ink and laboriously scratching the words. It was in someone else's handwriting. Hobson read it as best he could:

"1848. Her Majesty's Ships *Terror* and *Erebus* were deserted on the 22nd April 5 leagues NNW of this . . . been beset since 12th Sept. 1846. The officers & crews consisting of 105 souls under the command . . . F. R. M. Crozier landed here—in Latitude 69 degrees, 37 minutes, 42 seconds, and Longitude 98 degrees, 41 minutes.

"Paper was found by Lt. Irving under the cairn supposed to have been built by Sir James Ross in 1831, 4 miles to the northward, where it had been deposited by the late Commander Gore in June, 1847. Sir James Ross' pillar has not, however, been found, and the paper has been transferred to this position, which is that in which Sir J. Ross' pillar was erected.

"Sir John Franklin died on the 11th June, 1847, and the total loss by deaths in the Expedition has been to this date 9 officers & fifteen men."

Silence followed. Hobson slowly lifted his eyes from the paper and looked around the circle of faces. Each man must have been picturing in his mind those last days aboard the *Erebus* and *Terror,* both ships tossed on the ice, months stretching into years. In the summer of 1847 the ice never melted. Supplies ran low. Scurvy may have started.

Their commander had died that summer. Where he was buried, this last message did not say. Franklin's men knew only that their last hope lay in abandoning the ships and heading for the mainland.

As they traveled, hungry and weak, they discarded everything they could not carry. Here at Victory Point they left behind as many things as they could possibly spare. But where were they going?

"Here are the signatures," Hobson said, looking back at the paper. He read aloud: "James Fitzjames, Captain, Her Majesty's Ship *Erebus*. F. R. M. Crozier, Captain and Senior Officer, and start on tomorrow 26th for Back's Fish River."

This time when Hobson looked up, he said, "That's all."

The Eskimos had been right. The hungry and desperate men of Franklin's expedition had gone down toward the Great Fish River, or Back River. Judging from what John Rae and others had heard the Eskimos in that region say, the last survivors had fallen and died along the way.

Hobson's men went slowly back to work, sorting the clothing and looking for other traces of the expedition. Paper in hand, Lieutenant Hobson walked to the edge of Victory Point and looked out across Victoria Strait. For as far as he could see, the ocean was frozen in a solid mass of glistening white. The Arctic sky, nearly white itself, came down to join the horizon in a line that was hard to define in some places.

Out there the *Erebus* and *Terror* had come to rest. Out there they had been abandoned. Somewhere out there John Franklin had died. Hobson knew that before him stretched the final grave of the explorer whom the world had been seeking for more than a decade.

He looked at the paper again. On their first exploring party, Gore and Des Voeux must certainly have discovered that this wide sea beyond King William Island constituted the last link of the Northwest Passage. On discovering this, they must have hurried to the ship and informed their commander.

The message in the cylinder meant that Sir John

The *Erebus* in the ice, from an oil painting by Francois Musir

Franklin, after a life of hardship and privation in the Arctic, had finally discovered the object for which he had searched so many years and traveled so many thousands of miles. The Northwest Passage was his at last! He must have died with a smile of satisfaction on his face.

Twenty-six

THE ENDLESS QUEST

The cairn at Victory Point yielded the only official record of the expedition that has ever been found.

Why had the expedition failed? Why did every one of its men succumb before reaching help? No answers to these questions have ever been found, and perhaps none ever will. And yet there is an answer—a larger answer than perhaps John Franklin ever realized.

This was that the British expeditions of his day never met the Arctic on its own terms. They took their own civilized society with them—silverware, top hats, and all. They insisted on living as valiant British explorers had always lived on expeditions. Had they learned to live as Eskimos, to thrive off the land, to hunt by Indian methods, to make their clothes from animal skins—how different the story might have been. As it was, their food and supplies ran low, they left the shelter of their ships, and the Arctic conquered them.

But so dramatic and mysterious a disappearance was bound to grip the minds of men for decades after McClintock's voyage—and in fact still does.

Captain C. F. Hall, of Cincinnati, Ohio, landed on the northern shore of Hudson Bay in 1864 and spent five years with the Eskimos, searching for remains of the

Roald Amundsen

Franklin expedition. He found very little to add to what had already been discovered.

Captain Allen Young, who had been with McClintock, attempted to sail an old steam-powered man-of-war, the *Pandora,* through the Northwest Passage in 1875 but did not succeed.

In 1879 Lieutenant Frederick Schwatka, of the United States Army, camped with a small exploring party on King William Island. With the help of Eskimos they examined the island with utmost care, but made no major discoveries.

Meanwhile the Northeast Passage—across the top of Russia—was conquered that same year by Baron Nordenskiöld of Sweden, who traveled from that country direct to Bering Strait almost in a single season.

The Northwest Passage was finally navigated between 1903 and 1906 by a 29-year-old Norwegian explorer named Roald Amundsen, who six years later would become the first man to reach the South Pole. So small was his ship, the *Gjöa,* that it carried only six men. It scraped the rocks and darted in constant danger among the ice floes, but it succeeded, and the Northwest Passage was conquered at last.

The search for Franklin still goes on. At the urging of British Rear Admiral Noel Wright, the Spence Bay patrol of the Royal Canadian Mounted Police visited the west coast of Boothia in 1952 and the Adelaide Peninsula in 1955, without making significant discoveries.

But there are still places in that frozen land where no man has searched. Perhaps some day . . .

Lady Franklin lived to the age of eighty-three. After McClintock's return with news of her husband's fate she knew that her task was done. She had accomplished as much as a devoted wife could to honor the man she loved.

In later years she carefully gathered and saved every paper and possession of his, going as far back as his midshipman days on the *Polyphemus*—anything that would preserve his memory.

In Lincolnshire, John Franklin's fellow citizens erected a statue of him in the market square at Spilsby, his birthplace. The British Parliament voted two thousand pounds for erection of a monument in London, where it stands today with the inscription:

FRANKLIN
To the great navigator
and his brave companions
who sacrificed their lives
in completing the discovery
of the North-west Passage
A.D. 1847-48
Erected by the unanimous
vote of Parliament

National Memorial to
John Franklin in
Waterloo Place, London

One of Lady Franklin's final acts before her death in 1875 was to secure the installation of a marble tablet in the noblest shrine of all—Westminster Abbey. The plaque was unveiled in July of that year, and on it was an inscription by Lord Tennyson, the famed Poet Laureate of England and a nephew of Sir John by marriage. It read:

Not here! the white North hath thy bones, and thou
Heroic sailor soul,
Art passing on thy happier voyage now
Towards no earthly pole.

John Franklin shared some of the greatest adventures of all time—sailing with Flinders, fighting with Nelson, joining with Ross and Parry in the exploration of the Arctic, serving his fellow men in a time when honor and dignity and faith in God were the paramount requisites of fame.

Today his name is immortalized in many a geographic Northwest Passage of which, in the words of his friend Dr. Richardson, he and his gallant crews forged the last link with their lives.

FOR FURTHER READING

Andrist, Ralph K., *Heroes of Polar Exploration*, 1962, American Heritage, New York, N.Y.

Fitzpatrick, Kathleen, *Sir John Franklin in Tasmania*, 1949, Melbourne University Press, Victoria, Australia.

Flinders, Matthew, *A Voyage to Terra Australis*, 1814, Nicol, London, England.

Franklin, John, *Narrative of a Journey to the Shores of the Polar Sea*, 1823, Murray, London, England.

————, *Narrative of a Second Expedition to the Shores of the Polar Sea*, 1828, Murray, London, England.

Kirwan, L. P., *A History of Polar Exploration*, 1959, Norton, New York, N.Y.

McClintock, Leopold, *The Voyage of the "Fox,"* 1869, Murray, London, England.

Markham, Albert, *Life of Sir John Franklin*, c. 1875, Dodd, Mead and Co., New York, N.Y.

Scott, Ernest, *The Life of Captain Matthew Flinders*, 1914, Robertson, Sydney, Australia.

Stefansson, Viljhalmur, *Northwest to Fortune*, 1958, Duell, New York, N.Y.

Traill, H. D., *The Life of Sir John Franklin*, 1896, Murray, London, England.

Warner, Oliver, *Nelson and the Age of Fighting Sail*, 1963, American Heritage, New York, N.Y.

INDEX

Printed in U.S.A.